The Big Story: One Hope

SPRING HARVEST

Equipping the Church for action

Also available in Braille and Giant Print

Copyright © 2008 Spring Harvest

Russell Rook asserts the moral right to be identified as the author of this work.

Published by
Spring Harvest
14 Horsted Square
Uckfield
East Sussex TN22 1QG

First edition 2008

ISBN   978-1-899788-60-6

Acknowledgements
All Scripture quotations unless indicated otherwise taken from the HOLY
BIBLE, NEW INTERNATIONAL VERSION.
Copyright © 1973, 1978, 1984 by International Bible Society.
Used by permission of Hodder & Stoughton Publishers, a member of the
Hodder Headline Group.
All rights reserved. "NIV" is a registered trademark of International Bible
Society.
UK trademark number 1448790.

Scripture marked NRSV taken from NRSV *The New Revised Standard Version*
(Anglicized Edition), copyright 1989, 1995 by the Division of Christian
Education of the National Council of the Churches of Christ in the United
States of America. Used by permission. All rights reserved.

Please note that the inclusion of a quotation or example in this book does not
imply endorsement by Spring Harvest.

Spring Harvest. A Registered Charity.

THE BIG STORY
ONE
GOD
PEOPLE
HOPE
Celebrating the one true God

Spring Harvest 2008

STUDY GUIDE

by Russell Rook

The author would like to express his thanks to the following, who have all made valuable contributions to the Spring Harvest 2008 Study Guide.

Richard Bauckham, Sarah Doyle, Stephen Gaukroger, Sherri Golisky, Stephen Holmes, Adam Knuckey, Matt Little, Ernest Lucas, Ian Mayhew and the Spring Harvest Leadership Team: Pete Broadbent, Steve Chalke, Ian Coffey, Ruth Dearnley, Alan Johnson, Jeff Lucas and Rachael Orrell.

SPRING
HARVEST
Equipping the Church for action

contents

DAY 2 – ONE HOPE: on a hill   12

DAY 3 – ONE HOPE: in the garden   42

DAY 4 – ONE HOPE: out of town   68

DAY 5 – ONE HOPE: in the city   96

ONE HOPE
Introduction

The Big Story so far...

At Spring Harvest 2006, we began a three-year journey through *The Big Story*. As we have explored the grand narrative of Scripture, we have hoped and prayed for a fresh encounter with the one true God.

One God, One People, One Hope

Since the dawn of history, God's people have prayed the *Shema* as an act of devotion and witness. Most people in ancient times worshipped many gods, and the monotheism of Israel was distinctly different. Although unfashionable, Israel's position was simple; she prayed to the one true God, the world's only source of hope.

God made himself known to his people through stories, songs, poems, prayers, encounters and events. He instructed them to remember and retell his revelations for all eternity. They were to perform the all-singing, all-dancing narrative of the one true God daily. In this way, despite her many flaws and imperfections, Israel re-enacted God's story for the world. The climax was Jesus of Nazareth, who changed God's revelation to Israel into public property. Through Jesus, all creation finds its time, place and part in God's story.

In today's world nations continue to pay homage to many gods, but we, the people of the one true God, stand together and say: The Lord our God is one. We will love the Lord our God with all our heart and with all our soul and all our strength. And we will love our neighbour as ourselves.

The greatest eschatology act the world has ever seen

In this the final part of our trilogy, we approach the end of God's big story. In theological circles, this area is called *eschatology* – a word made by combining the Greek words *eschaton* (or *eschata*), meaning 'the end' (or 'things of the end'), and *logos,* meaning 'words'.

Christian eschatology is an attempt to find words to describe the end of all things, and in particular it is concerned with the famous four last things:

> Hear, O Israel: The LORD our God, the LORD is One. Love the LORD your God with all your heart and with all your soul and with all your strength.
> The Shema: Deuteronomy 6:4–5

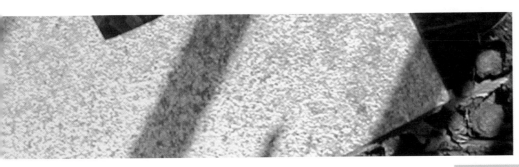

ONE
GOD
PEOPLE
HOPE
Celebrating the one true God

- THE SECOND COMING of Christ
- DEATH AND JUDGMENT
- THE RESURRECTION of the dead
- THE CREATION of a new heaven and earth.

Eschatology is what happens when we speak of our final hopes and tell the end of God's big story, and it is unashamedly Christological. The Bible identifies Jesus as the first and last above creation, the be-all and end-all of eschatology and the one true source of hope. Hence, in all our eschatological explorations we must endeavour to stick close to Jesus.

Eschatology attracts a certain type of Christian, while confusing or terrifying others. A recent telephone poll on a talk radio station in the United States suggests that over 30 per cent of Americans expect the second coming of Christ in their lifetime. Upon reflection, this statistic should be unsurprising. Ever since Christ's ascension, Christians have expected his imminent return. And who is to say they are wrong to live in hope and expectancy?

Regardless of any particular take on the end times, true Christian living is an experiment in eschatology and an exercise in hopefulness. Although there is much we do not know, we can be certain of what, or rather whom, we hope for. God created the world through Jesus, so too Jesus will determine its final end and its outcome.

There is far more to eschatology than a few theories concerning the nature, timing and results of the final battle. Eschatology is the church's attempt to account for God's activity and sovereignty within history. It is our attempt to make sense of God's good and perfect plans amidst the pain and suffering that surround us. It is our proclamation of God's kingdom in the fallen reality of our lives. In fact, Christian eschatology locates us simultaneously in the perfection of God's new creation and in this sin-soaked world. Living between these worlds is the uneasy reality for every disciple who ever lived.

Making detailed predictions concerning the exact time and place of Christ's return is an unavoidably speculative and spurious pastime. Given the journey ahead, whether or not we count ourselves with the expectant 30 per cent of Americans is largely irrelevant. The important thing is what we hope for. In the big story, hope is not an object to be owned or a timetable to be kept. Gospel hope is personal. We hope for Jesus. In him we discover God's sure and certain hope for creation. It is through Christ that we, God's people, become a foretaste of Christ's kingdom. As American pastor Bill Hybels is fond of saying, "The local church is the hope of the world."

ONE HOPE
INTRODUCTION

space for notes

Hope for yesterday, today, tomorrow

The book of Isaiah is our guide for the journey ahead. For both Israel and the church, Isaiah is an essential handbook on hope. The poems and songs in chapters 40 to 55 were not written to be rolled up in a scroll. They are to be sung and shouted. Isaiah is performance art for the Old Testament generation. It displays divine drama, and demands prophetic imagination and creative interaction. God's people were not given these words just to read, but to perform; and this they continue to do. Recitation of these passages is not merely an act of memory, a sentimental reminiscence of good days in the past.

The people featured in Isaiah 40–55 are a people under judgment, and throughout history reciting these chapters has brought new hope to life. Here we unveil the secret of prophecy – Isaiah is not only God's signpost to the future but also his means of changing the present. It's still true today. When we live prophetic lives, God's good and perfect will (his full and final future) invades the pain and problems of our present. Through many centuries Isaiah has enabled the faithful to hope and has brought something of God's beautiful tomorrow into their broken todays.

Contemporary scholarship has sparked many discussions over the date and authorship of Isaiah. Some view Isaiah as one volume by a single prophet, while others argue that it is three volumes written over several centuries by successive generations of prophets and poets. Whether we think Isaiah is the work of one prophet or a serial prophecy written by a team over several generations will depend largely on which scholars we side with. Thematically, at least, the book features three distinct main sections (chapters 1–39, 40–55 and 56–66). The second section, sometimes referred to as Second Isaiah, Exilic Isaiah or Deutero Isaiah, provides the biblical launch pad for the hopeful expedition and eschatological exploration that lie ahead.

Written for a time of darkness, these middle sixteen chapters comprise a masterful manual on hope. While the dating of the book is a matter of continued debate, few dispute that the prophecies were given to Israel as a message of hope during exile. What's more, generations of God's people can testify to God's Spirit speaking through the prophecies of Isaiah – regardless of their exact date or author.

Whether created with supernatural foresight or as a subversive response to the anguish of exile, these poems and songs are among the most profound prophecies. In them the light of God pierces one of Israel's darkest hours. Hundreds of miles from home, lost to her promised land and unable to attend temple, Israel finds new hope.

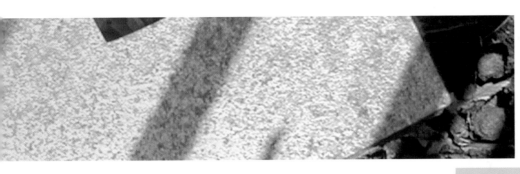

THE BIG STORY

ONE
GOD
PEOPLE
HOPE

Celebrating the one true God

For those brave enough to hold on to God's word, a new day was dawning. And with it came both the promise of homecoming and a transformed today for the Israelites in exile. Armed with hope in these trying times Israel would fulfil her calling to be God's people in new and daring ways. This chapter in the big story encompasses the birth of the synagogues; the documentation of large parts of the Old Testament story; the fulfilment of Israel's calling to be a light to the Gentiles; and the promise of a coming kingdom and a messiah and even advance copies of some of his greatest sermons.

The importance of these passages for future believers is just as inestimable as was its original impact. The words of Isaiah proved decisive in Jesus' ministry. Isaiah enabled the early church to understand the significance of Jesus' mission for the world. Isaiah continues to inspire the church to worship the King and manifest his kingdom today. In Christmas concerts and Easter services, in songs and symphonies, and in innumerable Sunday sermons, Isaiah continues to provide hope for today and tomorrow.

Recently, scholars have been asserting the prophetic relevance of Isaiah for the twenty-first century church. Christians in the West live in an increasingly foreign land. Where once the Christian worldview dominated, now we are a minority faith frequently misunderstood by the mainstream. Some of us, not unlike some Israelites in Babylon, are tempted to give up hoping. While others of us remain convinced that God's big story is the only hope for creation.

For these reasons, and in a bid to unlock God's hope in the past, present and future, we are setting out on our daily expeditions from the biblical base camp of Isaiah 40–55.

Where to start and how to go...

Before starting our journey through God's big story, Spring Harvest invited theologians and thinkers to prepare us for the road ahead. "If we are to really do justice to God's story," one commented, "we should begin with the Easter story and then return to the beginning to study the whole narrative in the light of Christ." With the help of Isaiah, we will do precisely that. Here, in these prophetic passages, the whole of God's story awaits us.

There are four stages in the journey ahead.

- DAY TWO: Hope on a Hill (Isaiah 52:13 – 53:12)
  Christ and his gospel, the story around which all of creation is centred and within which history finds its ultimate climax and fulfilment.

- DAY THREE: Hope in the Garden (Isaiah 40)

  The story of creation, the epic that is the basis of all else. Here, in the very beginnings of the universe, we shall begin to discover God's hopes for his creation.

- DAY FOUR: Hope out of Town (Isaiah 42:21 – 44:5)

  The Exodus, the story that unlocks the secret to faith and hope. In the big story, every previous divine intervention points towards a new future and every memory of what God has done is a promise of what is to come.

- DAY FIVE: Hope in the City (Isaiah 55)

  The finale, the Bible's vision of a new heaven and a new earth and God's plan to make all things new.

Our prayer is that all who join us on the journey discover the hope that God has for his people and his creation. Hope is our belief in, and commitment to, a better tomorrow. It is the very possibility of a future tense, a prayer and a promise for God's coming kingdom.

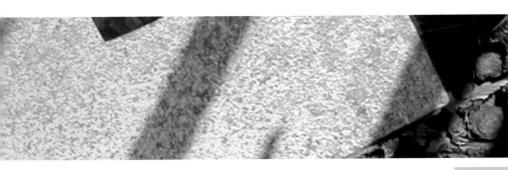
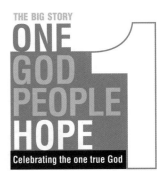

THE BIG STORY

ONE
GOD
PEOPLE
HOPE

Celebrating the one true God

2 ONE HOPE ON A HILL

Hope on a hill
Introduction

The way ahead

God's story is filled with surprises, but few surpass the events of Easter. An innocent man brutally beaten by a bloodthirsty crowd, the saviour of the world mistaken for public enemy number one. On that hill far away we glimpse the climax of history and the salvation of the world. Hopes and fears meet in these remarkable and surprising events.

Today, we will revisit the events of the first Easter from three perspectives.

1. ISAIAH: We will reflect upon Christ's life, death and resurrection through the prophecy of Isaiah.

2. THE DISCIPLES: We will discuss the impact of these events on his followers.

3. THE CHURCH: We will consider what it means for us to live as the community of the resurrection.

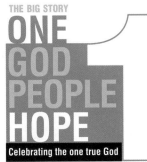

THE BIG STORY
ONE
GOD
PEOPLE
HOPE
Celebrating the one true God

Teaching Block 1:

The King Surprising

In Teaching Block 1 we will explore…

- The new day that comes with Christ's incarnation.
- The unique qualities of kingship which we find in Jesus.
- The coronation of Jesus as the King of the World.

Teaching Block 2:

The King Rising

In Teaching Block 2 we will reflect upon…

- The resurrection of Jesus as God's vindication and victory in human history.
- The implications of the resurrection for Christ's followers.
- The ongoing power of the resurrection in the church and the world.

2 ONE HOPE ON A HILL

Teaching Block 1:

The king surprising

1.1
A promising king

In Scripture, a new king begins a new era for his people. It is no coincidence that Isaiah's first vision comes soon after the death of the king. There is a new king on the throne and a new prophet in town. This can only mean one thing: a new day is dawning.

> In the year that King Uzziah died, I saw the Lord…
>
> Isaiah 6:1

In some ways, not much has changed. People who saw the coronation of Queen Elizabeth II proudly recall witnessing the beginning of a new reign. In 1997 the Labour Party swept into government to the lyrics 'things can only get better.' The campaign theme song blared out at every husting and New Labour won a landslide election victory.

Charged with hope, Isaiah promises a new day for God's people. Exiled in a strange and foreign land, they welcome his news. But what kind of day is dawning? It surely is more than just *another* day. If the next day is the same as the last then there is no hope. When Isaiah speaks of a *new* day, what does he mean?

> From now on I will tell you of new things, of hidden things unknown to you. They are created now, and not long ago; you have not heard of them before today.
>
> Isaiah 48:6b–7

The Hebrew word he uses is *chadash*, which can mean several things. In certain instances it refers to more of the same. The accession of Elizabeth II to the throne provides a perfect example of this. Her coronation confirmed Elizabeth as the next monarch in a long line of succession. And while her rule has been marked by changing attitudes to the monarchy, she has essentially fulfilled the same constitutional role.

> The book of Isaiah, however, is not simply a telling of the political story of Judah, nor of the sequence of superpowers. It is not in the end an act of political theory or history. What makes this rendering of Judah's life distinctive is that the story is told with unfailing attentiveness to Yahweh, who is reckoned to be the primal player.
>
> Walter Brueggemann, *Isaiah 40–66 Vol 2* (Westminster Bible Companion), (Westminster/John Knox Press, 1998)

In another context, *chadash* designates a totally *new* type of newness. Here, the new thing is not just the next same thing but a qualitatively different thing. This kind of newness doesn't just replace the old, it surpasses it.

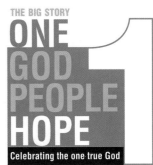

Story of Hope:

This is history

I remember being eight-years-old and watching the coronation on a friend of my parents' nine inch television. I was playing outside on a sunny day in Derby, until my mother called me in and said: "This is history, come and see the Queen being crowned". There must have been about twenty people crowded into this small room waiting for the moment that the Queen was crowned.

Rosina Rowland, comment made at: http://news.bbc.co.uk/ onthisday/hi/witness/june/2/newsid_2947000/2947912.stm

Hope Quote:

Who's the king?

When Jesus proclaimed the coming of the kingdom of God he is declaring that 'the time has come' for God to reassert his rule over the world (Mark 1:14–15). Moreover he is hinting that he himself is God's king, a fact borne out by his authority over people, spirits, sickness and sin (Mark 1:16 – 2:12) as well as over nature and death (Mark 4:35 – 5:43).

Tim Chester, "The Kingdom of God is at Hand: Eschatology and Mission" in Stephen Holmes & Russell Rook (eds.), *What Are We Waiting For?* (Paternoster, Milton Keynes, 2008)

Hope Note:

Technological advances

Technological advances are either adaptive or disruptive. The Sony Walkman® is an iconic example of adaptive technology. By producing a much smaller personal cassette player, Sony Corporation created a new product. The Walkman was new in one sense of the word. Apple's iPod®, however, is a disruptive technology. It is not merely an advance over an existing machine but is an altogether new type of technology. The iPod was new in the sense of the word that Isaiah uses to describe God's future for Israel.

Hope Quote:

Revolution

"Every revolutionary ends up either by becoming an oppressor or a heretic."

Albert Camus (1913–1960, French existential writer)

2 ONE HOPE
ON A HILL

Comment: "[Isaiah's] Transcendent newness… look[s] forward to the unprecedented act of salvation… that God is about to perform. This will be something unheard of before. It will so surpass even God's great acts of salvation in Israel's past."

Richard Bauckham & Trevor Hart, *Hope Against Hope: Christian Eschatology at the Turn of the Millennium* (Eerdmans, Grand Rapids, 1999), 78

"Look, my servant will prosper, will rise to great heights… . Nations will be astonished and kings will stay tight-lipped before him, seeing what had never been told them, learning what they had not learned before."

Isaiah 52:13, 15, cited in Daniel Berrigan (tr.), *Isaiah: Spirit of Courage, Gift of Tears* (Augsburg Fortress, Minneapolis, 1996) 141

Just as there were many who were appalled at him – his appearance was so disfigured beyond that of any man and his form marred beyond human likeness – so will he sprinkle many nations, and kings will shut their mouths because of him. For what they were not told, they will see, and what they have not heard, they will understand. Who has believed our message and to whom has the arm of the LORD been revealed? He grew up before him like a tender shoot, and like a root out of dry ground. He had no beauty or majesty to attract us to him, nothing in his appearance that we should desire him.

Isaiah 52:14 – 53:2

The poetry of Isaiah specialises in this kind of newness. In fact, between Isaiah 40 and 66 we find more examples of this radical, transcendent, life-changing newness than are in the entire rest of the Bible. It says here that Israel's bright new day will begin with raising up God's servant. He will be high and exalted above all history and creation. Other rulers, whether godly or ungodly, benevolent or despotic, will be silenced by his majestic presence. He will break their silence by uttering truths that no king could utter.

This is not the routine coronation of a would-be king. It is the triumphant entry of a new kind of ruler. But who could reign in this way?

History shows that kings such as this are hard to find. Time and again, we raise our hopes only to be disappointed by the new ruler's flaws, frailties and failures. Certain subjects and members of the electorate will testify to similar frustrations with the rule of Queen Elizabeth II, or the leadership of Tony Blair. Having taken power, the new guard often repeats the old guard's mistakes. It's been this way throughout time and history. When politics takes place in the middle of the road, we bemoan a lack of new ideas. But when revolution is rife, the new ideas rarely survive long. Hence, our hopes for a truly *new* day rest on the arrival of a truly *new* kind of king.

1.2
A king arriving

It never ceases to surprise us how so many people, having waited for so long, missed God's new day when it came. Tens of thousands recognised Jesus as the Messiah, but many more did not. How can people who have been praying so hard for the Messiah to come miss him so easily when he arrives? The answer is simply that he didn't look like the promised one. If he was the king that Israel was waiting for, why didn't he look more like royalty?

However, God's people were not without warning. Isaiah, for example, went out of his way to highlight the surprising nature of God's promised one. Only once is Israel's Messiah described as a king. The exalted one is first, and foremost, a servant. His status comes not from his appearance but from the one he serves.

God's servant king is full of surprises, but here we will explore three in particular. The first we have just mentioned. He claims to be the king of the Jews, but Jesus appears remarkably un-royal. The background of God's chosen one is unexceptional and his physical appearance is un-majestic, even unattractive.

THE BIG STORY

ONE
GOD
PEOPLE
HOPE

Celebrating the one true God

1

Hope Note:

A new day?

In *Lonely Planet Guide to England*, David Elsie writes: "In 1997 … 'New' Labour swept to power with a record parliamentary majority, under a fresh-faced new leader called Tony Blair. After nearly 18 years of Conservative rule, it really seemed that Labour's victory call ('things can only get better') was true – and some people literally danced in the street when the results were announced."

There are times when we glimpse the spirit of Christ's new-style kingship in earthly leaders who not only raise the hopes of their people for 'a new day' but start to deliver on them too. Nelson Mandela's imprisonment may, ironically, have been the key that enabled him to lead differently. Separated from the political machine for the best part of three decades, Mandela embodied a decisive break with the previous way of doing things. In an interview in *Vanity Fair* (July 2007, page 168) titled "A Man Called Hope," former President Bill Clinton asked President Mandela whether he hated those who had imprisoned him for 27 years. Mandela replied, "Of course I felt old anger rising up again, and fear... . But I knew that,… if I continued to hate them, they would still have me. I wanted to be free, and so I let it go."

Hope in Verse:

Indifference

When Jesus came to Birmingham they simply passed Him by,
They never hurt a hair of Him, they only let Him die;
     Geoffrey Anketell Studdert Kennedy, *Rhymes* (Hodder and
Stoughton, 1929): 43. 1929 (7) 3853 Cambridge University Library

Scenes of Hope:

Children of men

The Children of Men is a dystopian novel by P. D. James that is set in a world in which, 18 years previously, babies suddenly and inexplicably stopped being born. No longer hearing children's voices, the population is paralysed with apathy, pessimism and despair.

Hope comes into this darkening world in the form of a pregnant woman named Kee. In the film adaptation (directed by Alfonso Cuarón 2006), Theo Faron is tasked with taking Kee and her baby to safety through a war zone.

With a battle raging around them, Theo leads Kee and her newborn child cautiously down the stairwell of a tower block. When the soldiers and terrorists catch sight of the baby in Kee's arms, the fighting stops. In this instance a newborn brings momentary peace to a war torn world. In the gospel, a baby brings eternal peace to a dying world.

2 ONE HOPE ON A HILL

> Your attitude should be the same as that of Christ Jesus: Who, being in very nature God, did not consider equality with God something to be grasped, but made himself nothing, taking the very nature of a servant, being made in human likeness. And being found in appearance as a man, he humbled himself and became obedient to death – even death on a cross! Therefore God exalted him to the highest place and gave him the name that is above every name, that at the name of Jesus every knee should bow, in heaven and on earth and under the earth, and every tongue confess that Jesus Christ is Lord, to the glory of God the Father.
>
> Philippians 2:5–11

Comment: "As the chosen servant, God 'became a beggar on earth, in order that we might become rich from his poverty'."
Cyril of Alexandria, cited in Robert Louis Wilken (ed. trans.), *Isaiah: Interpreted by Early Christian and Medieval Commentators* (Eerdmans, 2007), 416

Rather than being regally aloof, the one for whom Israel waits is immersed in the painful realities of daily life.

While he looks like the lowest of the low, Jesus actually carries God's power within. It is impossible to resist the church's conviction that Jesus is the fulfilment of Israel's hope, Isaiah's long-awaited servant and the carrier of the kingdom. The Son of God sets aside his heavenly position in order to serve his own creatures. His world-changing humility is not a one-off event, nor a display of deference by the creator condescending to undergo work experience. It is Christ's willingness to be despised and rejected, to embrace suffering and sorrow, that authenticates him as God's true servant. What's more, his willingness to give up divine status and serve the world is what makes him in very nature God.

The life of a servant exposes common misconceptions of divinity with the startling reality of who God actually is. He makes a mockery of the kings of antiquity, who exalted themselves to semi-divine status. Likewise, our own attempts at social climbing look foolish in the light of Christ's counter-cultural kingship. God does not demand worship in order to reinforce his supernatural ego, but wins the worship of the heavens and the earth through his willingness to serve and save.

The gospel story calls on every generation anew to rethink its concept of God. Like Israel, we face the fact that Jesus is everything we hoped for but nothing like we expected. When we commend Christ to others we must be quick to warn them that while he's everything they need, he's unlike anything they've ever imagined. Moments when we feel that Jesus is being misrepresented should provide us with some encouragement. The reason some people struggle to understand Jesus is because he is beyond popular portrayal. The challenge to those of us who have encountered Jesus in his word is to play our part in presenting the facts and dispelling the fallacies.

Despite all we read in Isaiah, the incarnation remains thoroughly surprising and possible to miss. The Son of God in a body of flesh and serving mankind is such a radical notion it is almost unthinkable and unimaginable. And yet this is the gospel story. Jesus is born not in a palace, but among animals. He rides into Jerusalem not as a warlord on a stallion, but in peace on a donkey. He does not enlist soldiers to march on Rome, but washes the feet of his followers and invites them to share his table. And he refuses a throne and casts aside the crown of conventional kingship.

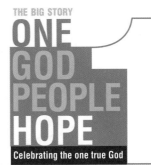

Re-definition

The [Church] Fathers realised that the incarnation demanded a rethinking of the meaning of the word God.

Colin Gunton, *Yesterday and Today* (Eerdmans 1983)

Hope Quote:

Lord of the Rings

All that is gold does not glitter,

Not all those who wander are lost;

The old that is strong does not wither,

Deep roots are not reached by the frost.

From the ashes a fire shall be woken,

A light from the shadows shall spring;

Renewed shall be blade that was broken,

The crownless again shall be king.

JRR Tolkien, *The Fellowship of the Ring*

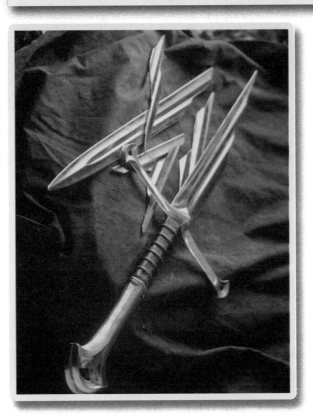

Hope in Verse:

Jesus of the Scars

If we have never sought, we seek Thee now;

Thine eyes burn through the dark, our only stars;

We must have sight of thorn-pricks on Thy brow,

We must have Thee, O Jesus of the Scars.

The heavens frighten us; they are too calm;

In all the universe we have no place.

Our wounds are hurting us; where is the balm?

Lord Jesus, by Thy Scars we claim Thy grace.

If, when the doors are shut, Thou drawest near,

Only reveal those hands, that side of Thine;

We know to-day what wounds are, have no fear,

Show us Thy Scars, we know the countersign.

The other gods were strong; but Thou wast weak;

They rode, but Thou didst stumble to a throne;

But to our wounds only God's wounds can speak,

And not a god has wounds, but Thou alone.

Edward Shillito (1872–1962)

2 ONE HOPE ON A HILL

1.3
A king dying

> He was despised and rejected by men, a man of sorrows, and familiar with suffering. Like one from whom men hide their faces he was despised, and we esteemed him not. Surely he took up our infirmities and carried our sorrows, yet we considered him stricken by God, smitten by him, and afflicted. But he was pierced for our transgressions, he was crushed for our iniquities; the punishment that brought us peace was upon him, and by his wounds we are healed. We all, like sheep, have gone astray, each of us has turned to his own way; and the Lord has laid on him the iniquity of us all. He was oppressed and afflicted, yet he did not open his mouth; he was led like a lamb to the slaughter, and as a sheep before her shearers is silent, so he did not open his mouth.
>
> Isaiah: 53:3–7

Comment: Of the many passages of Isaiah which Jesus uses in his life and ministry, Isaiah 53 is of particular importance. The idea that the suffering of one person might have redemptive power in the life of God's people had been common since the exile and recent events had increased this surprising hope.

> He was assigned a grave with the wicked, and with the rich in his death, though he had done no violence, nor was any deceit in his mouth. Yet it was the Lord's will to crush him and cause him to suffer, and though the Lord makes his life a guilt offering, he will see his offspring and prolong his days, and the will of the Lord will prosper in his hand.
>
> Isaiah 53:9–10

Christ's death is the starkest fulfilment of Isaiah's poetry. Here is the second surprise: Not only is the king of the world the servant of all, but he is crowned on Good Friday. His death on a cross is the moment that defines the new day. With nothing but some wood and a few nails the servant king, the one who trained in a carpenter's workshop, initiates his rule and comes into his kingdom. Rejecting the bejewelled paraphernalia of Herod's palace and resisting any calls to chase the Roman oppressors out of town, Jesus gives up every bit of power and glory. He chooses a wreath of sharp thorns for a crown, the agony of the *Via Dolorosa* (Way of Grief) for his kingly procession, the anguished cry of dereliction for his coronation prayer and these words for his inaugural address: "Father, forgive them, for they do not know what they are doing." (Luke 23:34) On a hill, God's suffering servant is crowned king of the world.

The implications are monumental for those willing to witness the crucifixion, whether under the blackened Golgotha sky, on the wall of an art gallery or in an intense personal experience. We come close to Isaiah. As onlookers of the cross we join Isaiah, Ezekiel, John and other prophets in the throne room of God. From now on, whenever someone asks who God is or what he is like we can point to Jesus enthroned on a cross. This is the coronation of our God, the servant king. In a world that fails to see the God in front of its eyes, Isaiah's poem should be shouted to the ends of the earth.

Jesus was the king that Israel had been hoping for, but he died. Although we said Isaiah was a book of hope, we read now some of the most tragic verses in the Bible. Isaiah 53:9–10 tells how the one who was hoped for appears to fall into the pit of hopelessness. So what's the use of a saviour if he can't even save himself? If God's promised servant is doomed to death, what hope is there for the living?

Israel's concept of life after death was far from certain. Theories ranged from God's people living on in the lives of their descendants (so infertility was considered a curse), to more developed accounts of resurrection. The Old Testament can be read as an extended account of the struggle between life and death. At the time of Christ, resurrection was the hot theory. With large numbers having been martyred while defending the promised land, the nation expected God's intervention or vindication. However, while many were hopeful that it might provide the answer, they knew resurrection would only become possible if God could do away with death.

space for notes

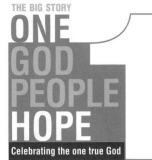
Scenes of Hope:

To end all wars

Captain Ernest Gordon of the Argyll and Sutherland Highlanders was the dean of the chapel of Princeton University for 26 years. He was converted and experienced his call to ministry in a Japanese prisoner of war camp, where captured soldiers were used as slave labour to build the infamous Thailand-Burma Railroad. Eighty thousand of them perished from cruelty and torture. As an officer, Gordon struggled to help his men make sense of all the suffering they had to endure. He became deathly ill, however, but was spared by the care of "Dusty Miller", who shared his own precious rations with Gordon. At one point, as Miller nursed Gordon's broken body back to health he spoke the words that would nurse Gordon's broken soul back to health and initiate his call into ministry. Miller told him: 'A man can experience an incredible amount of pain and suffering if he has hope. When he loses his hope, that's when he dies.' The story of Gordon and the men who built the bridge on the River Kwai is recorded in the film *To End All Wars* (2001). The film is based on the book *Miracle on the River Kwai* (also published as *Through the Valley of the Kwai*).

Poem of Hope:

A Better Resurrection
(extract)

I have no wit, I have no words, no tears;
My heart within me like a stone
Is numb'd too much for hopes or fears;
Look right, look left, I dwell alone;
I lift mine eyes, but dimm'd with grief
No everlasting hills I see;
My life is in the falling leaf;
O Jesus, quicken me.

Christina Rossetti (1830–1894 English poet)

Hope Quote:

Comforting those who mourn

When someone dies, most people retreat into an embarrassed silence; they can only shake the relatives warmly by the hand. There is nothing more one can 'do'. People don't mourn any more either, not because they don't want to, but because mourning rituals are obsolete, and no longer learnt. In public life the mourner has no status. Women no longer wear black, and men are no longer seen with black armbands. 'Life goes on': that is the only comfort. It seems as if the dying and the grieving would like to apologize – 'please don't let me be in your way' – and disappear from sight.

Jürgen Moltmann, *The Coming of God* (Augsburg Fortress 2004)

2 ONE HOPE ON A HILL

space for notes

Comment: "In death Jesus perfects all that he was sent to do, … The God who so loved the world that he gave his only Son is now revealed to all who gaze upon the one who has laid down his life for his friends, the greatest gesture of love possible. The central scene stands alone. It is devoted to Jesus' proclamation and coronation as King, and the ironic judgment of those who appear to be judging."

Francis J. Moloney, *Glory not Dishonour: Reading John 13–21* (Augsburg Fortress, Minneapolis, 1998)

… and he [Jesus] drove out the spirits with a word and healed all the sick. This was to fulfil what was spoken through the prophet Isaiah: "He took up our infirmities and carried our diseases."

Matthew 8:16–17

Comment: "The trouble is that God's people are… as good as dead, like the people in exile … resembling the bones of a corpse left to be picked bare by vultures, totally cut off, hopeless."

John Goldingay, "Eschatology in Isaiah" in Stephen Holmes & Russell Rook (eds.), *What Are We Waiting For?* (Paternoster Press, Milton Keynes, 2008)

From that time on Jesus began to explain to his disciples that he must go to Jerusalem and suffer many things…

Matthew 16:21

Yet it was the LORD's will to crush him and cause him to suffer, and though the LORD makes his life a guilt offering, he will see his offspring and prolong his days, and the will of the LORD will prosper in his hand.

Isaiah 53:10

Comment: "By the death of his own flesh, he destroyed death (Heb 2:14)."

Cyril of Alexandria, cited in Robert Louis Wilken (ed. trans.), *Isaiah: Interpreted by Early Christian and Medieval Commentators* (Eerdmans, 2007), 416

Views on the afterlife differed, but there was one consistent hope – God would ultimately win this battle. Christians pin their hopes for victory on the death and resurrection of Jesus, who surprised the world by choosing execution for a coronation and dying in a bid for eternal life. God's chosen servant defeated death, but not by dodging it, denying it or activating a divine get-out clause. Jesus absorbed death into his eternal life and in innocence took on all the sin, disease, suffering and pain that history threw at him. He obliterated death by allowing death to obliterate him.

Most people are desperate to evade death. We buy life insurance, gym membership, superfoods, private medical care and plastic surgery in a bid to remain longer on earth. When we can't avoid death due to the passing of a friend or relative, we charge through the experience with only a brief pause to mourn. And yet all life advances toward death. Our awareness of death is, in part, what makes us human. It marks us out from animals.

Isaiah is clear that God's servant is marked out for death, so Jesus knows what the cost of serving God will be. While others flee death, Jesus confronts it. He stares death down from the vantage point of the cross. His coronation is the moment in which he shares the worst pain and suffering that the world can inflict. It is when Jesus defeats death and earns the right to rule the world.

Religions and worldviews must at some point account for death, and none deals with the subject as powerfully, practically and profoundly as the gospel. God does not stare down from heaven wondering what mortality and mourning are like. He joins us, shares our grief and empathises in our sorrow. He knows better than any of us what death can do. God has died, in Jesus, and lived to tell the tale. For this reason he is the only one who can give hope to people walking in the valley of the shadow of death.

Story of Hope:

9/11

Will Jimeno and John McLoughlin were the last two people rescued from the World Trade Centre following the 11 September 2001 terrorist attack.

Jimeno, McLoughlin and three other Port Authority Police officers entered the underground concourse on a mission to rescue as many civilians as possible, but almost as soon as they got inside Tower Two collapsed, pinning McLoughlin and Jimeno under large blocks of concrete rubble and twisted steel and killing their three colleagues instantly.

For the next ten hours, Jimeno and his partner fought through pain and thirst inside a cramped concrete tomb swirling with dust and smoke. At times, ruptured gas lines would send fire balls hurtling into the collapsed ruins, threatening to burn the two men to death. In another terrifying moment, heat from the fireballs 'cooked off' the ammunition inside the firearm of a fallen officer, sending 15 bullets ricocheting around the chamber. At that point, Jimeno's hope began to falter.

"We had been crushed, burnt and shot by then," he says. "I was exhausted. I had done everything as a police officer that I could do, and everything as a human being. I was at that point where I just knew I was going to die."

Yet when things began to seem unbearable, Jimeno saw a figure coming towards him through the rubble.

"He wore a glowing white robe and a rope belt," he says. "I couldn't see his face, but I knew it was Jesus."

Jimeno saw an endless sea of waving grass over the figure's left shoulder and a lake over the right.

"I remember asking Jesus, 'If I get to heaven, can I have some water?'"

The vision filled him with hope.

"I had this resurgence of optimism, this resurgence of the will to fight," he says.

Turning toward McLoughlin, he yelled, 'We're going to get out of this hell-hole!' And they did. Several hours later, Marines and NYPD rescue workers lifted him out of his temporary prison, and Jimeno thanked God.

adapted from Mike Clark, "Living with a Wonderful Expectation," sermon delivered on Easter Sunday, April 8, 2007
http://www.unionpc.org/clark/Bible%20Messages/2007/Wonderful%20Expectations.htm

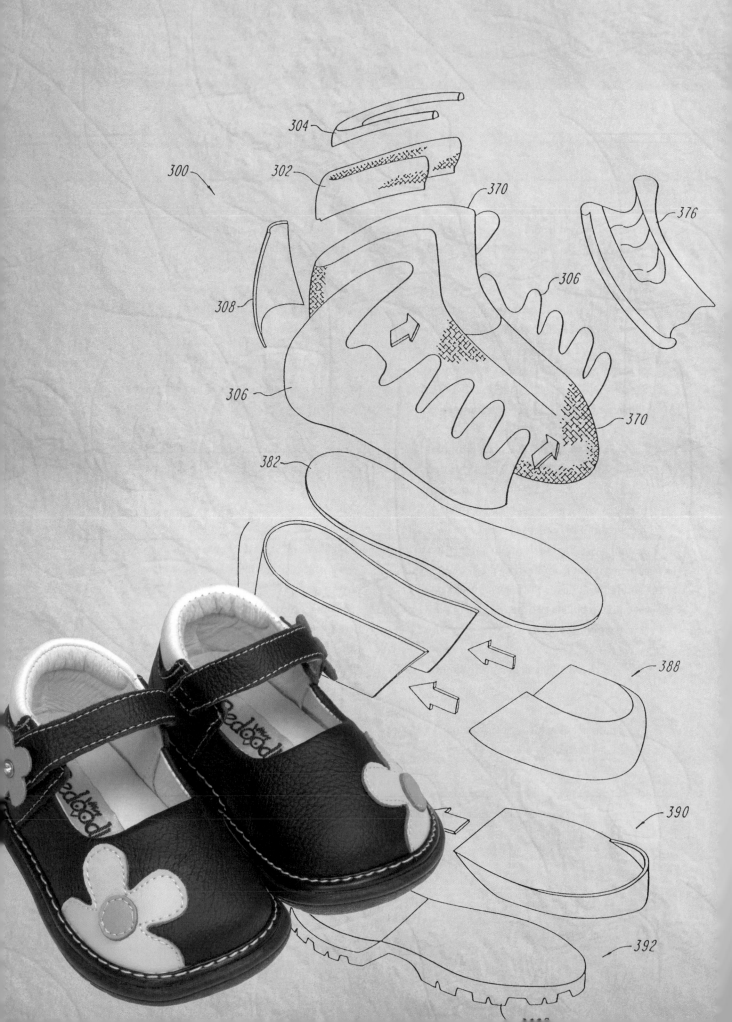

Shoes

Take off one of your shoes

We live in a world where death and its effects are an ever-present reality. As disciples of a God who confronts death head-on, we should not fear death.

Yet, in our weakness, there are many things that Christians might still fear, and therefore may well demonstrate despair instead of hope.

What prevents you from bringing hope and resurrection to your family, community and place of work or education? More specifically, which lies have you believed about yourself that prevent you from fully believing the hope that Jesus embodies?

Using a permanent marker, write these things on the sole of your shoe. Then put your shoe back on.

Over the course of the day, the natural process of walking around will erase these words from the bottom of your shoe. In this way, it becomes symbolic of a commitment to seeing these lies eradicated from your life.

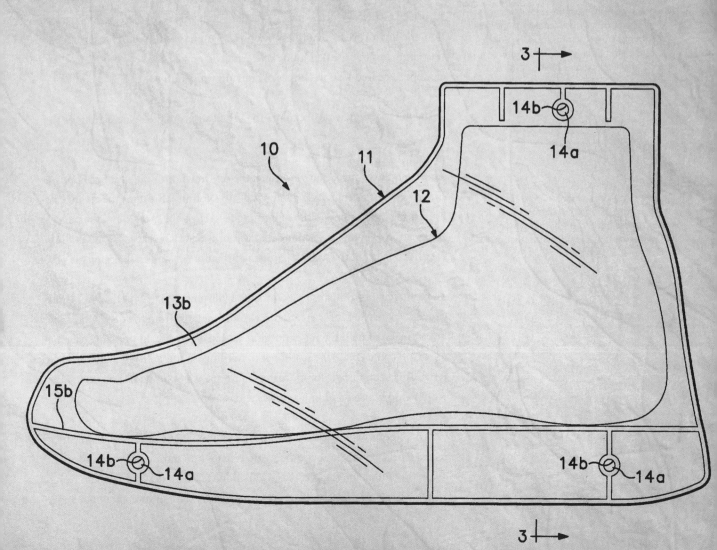

Teaching Block 2:

The king rising

2.1
He's alive

> After the suffering of his soul, he will see the light of life and be satisfied; by his knowledge my righteous servant will justify many, and he will bear their iniquities. Therefore I will give him a portion among the great, and he will divide the spoils with the strong, because he poured out his life unto death, and was numbered with the transgressors. For he bore the sin of many, and made intercession for the transgressors.
>
> Isaiah 53:11–12

As with many great works of literature, in Isaiah the greatest twist in the story is left until last. The parallels with the gospel are here for all to see. Having already surprised us twice, with a servant-shaped king who is crowned by public execution, the finale reveals that the suffering servant has returned to life. Crucifixion was not defeat but the beginning of eternal victory. At the very moment when all hope appeared lost, the hopes of creation were fulfilled.

In the next section, we will explore the implications of the resurrection for the world.

Above all, the resurrection vindicated the one in whom Israel put her hope. In the Old Testament, God's enemy is death. Nothing threatens the creator of everything like the possibility of nothingness. He is the great 'I am', the personification of being. Everything that was or is or will be exists because of him. Death is an affront to God, jeopardising his authority and challenging his power.

> Comment: "Ezekiel envisioned God turning these bones into corpses and the corpses back into a living army, and Isaiah envisages a similar resuscitation."
> John Goldingay, "Eschatology in Isaiah" in Stephen Holmes & Russell Rook (eds.), *What Are We Waiting For?* (Paternoster Press, Milton Keynes, 2008)

The resurrection confirms that God's life is all-powerful. Neither sin nor death can destroy his hopes for creation. By restoring Jesus from the dead God shows he can make something out of nothing, he can create life. In the same way that only God could create the world out of nothing, so too only God could resurrect Jesus. This is important for ultimately our hope is not found in Scripture, but within God himself and in his power and purpose.

Christian hope begins with the resurrection. It is characterised by the resurrected Christ. God's hope for the world crosses into our lives through the life of another human being. In Jesus, God's hope takes on flesh and we can relate to it, grasp it and understand it. For some, the thought of investing hope in

THE BIG STORY

ONE
GOD
PEOPLE
HOPE

1

Celebrating the one true God

Hope Note:

The resurrection in art

During the Second World War many of the priceless works of art in the National Gallery in London were removed for safe-keeping. Due to many requests, the gallery agreed to bring back certain pieces for limited periods according to public demand. At the height of the Blitz, the people of London overwhelmingly voted for the work *Noli me Tangere* (painted by Titian about 1514) to be returned to the gallery. The picture of Mary Magdalene and the resurrected Christ in the garden provided great hope at a time when hope appeared in short supply. Its title *noli me tangere* translates as 'let no one touch me', Jesus' words to Mary in John 20:14–18. In a war torn city only resurrection can bring lasting hope.

Poem of Hope:

Easter hymn

Death and darkness get you packing,
Nothing now to man is lacking.
All your triumphs now are ended,
And what Adam marred is mended.

Henry Vaughan (1621–1695)

image: FreeDigitalPhotos.net

Stories of Hope

No fear

David Watson in his book *Fear No Evil* recounts his personal struggle with cancer and reconciling his faith in the light of such suffering. In the final chapter, he writes:

"If we think of all of the best and most glorious moments in our lives, the perfection of what we experience always seems just beyond our reach. As with striking a succession of matches to light a dark room, those moments invariably seem to flicker and fade. Heaven will be like turning on the full light. The perfection will be there for us to enjoy, undefiled, unflickering and unfading. 'And the city had no need of sun or moon to shine upon it, for the glory of God is its light…' (Rev. 21:23). Here is the summit of all our highest hopes and dreams.

"In one sense, the Christian is not preparing for death. Essentially he is preparing for life, abundant life in all its fullness. The world, with all its fleeting pleasures, is not the final reality, with heaven as shadowy and suspect unknown. The best and purest joys on earth are only a shadow of the reality that God has prepared for us in Christ."

David C.K. Watson, *Fear No Evil: One Man Deals With Terminal Illness* (Harold Shaw 1985)

space for notes

Comment: "He over-turned destruction, and he fashions anew those overpowered by death so that they become incorruptible. He makes those on earth citizens of heaven and, through himself, unites those who had long ago strayed to God the Father. He proclaims release to the captives, recovery of sight to the blind (Isa 61:1). He heals the broken hearted. He emptied Hades and freed them from Satan's oppressive rule."

Cyril of Alexandria, cited in Robert Louis Wilken (ed. trans.), *Isaiah: Interpreted by Early Christian and Medieval Commentators* (Eerdmans, 2007), 416

How beautiful on the mountains are the feet of those who bring good news, who proclaim peace, who bring good tidings, who proclaim salvation, who say to Zion, "Your God reigns!" Listen! Your watchmen lift up their voices; together they shout for joy. When the LORD returns to Zion, they will see it with their own eyes. Burst into songs of joy together, you ruins of Jerusalem, for the LORD has comforted his people, he has redeemed Jerusalem. The LORD will lay bare his holy arm in the sight of all nations, and all the ends of the earth will see the salvation of our God.

Isaiah 52:7–11

Even after Jesus had done all these miraculous signs in their presence, they still would not believe him. This was to fulfil the word of Isaiah the prophet: "Lord, who has believed our message and to whom has the arm of the Lord been revealed?"

John 12:37–38

another human being may appear foolish. We have all placed hope in another person and been let down. However, while Jesus' humanity brings accessibility, his divinity brings immunity against the consequences of the fall. In Jesus we discover God's hope in and for humanity.

Jesus is an historical character, but he is unlike any other character in history. While we can learn from the lives of Alexander the Great, Martin Luther and Mother Theresa, these inspirational figures are no longer with us. Jesus, on the other hand, came back from the dead and is with us here and now. He is both a character from history and a character in our history; the subject of our hope yesterday, today and forever. He continues to share with us, speak to us and surprise us.

Jesus' death and resurrection brought the new day that creation was waiting for. It made something that appeared impossible, possible. We can know his resurrection power and share his eternal life. Our greatest fear has been erased and our hope has been born to eternal life.

2.2
The future's bright

In the resurrection, Israel's hunch that her story would not end in death was shown to be correct. For almost two thousand years since, the Christian rendition of hope has commenced with a retelling of the Easter story. The life, death and resurrection of Jesus marks the fulfilment of the Old Testament, a new day in history and the beginning of the end.

As the central figure in human history, Jesus is in a position to guide and direct history. He decides the world's future, embodies the new creation and proves God's power to grant life in all situations. From this exalted position, he imparts eternal life to those who place their hope in him. In Christ we find a sure and certain hope of an eternal future. Our hope for life beyond the grave is not

THE BIG STORY

ONE
GOD
PEOPLE
HOPE

1

Celebrating the one true God

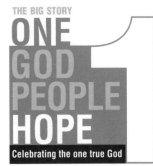

Hope in Verse:

The poisoned pool

Rob Lacey (1962–2006) gives a fantastic and creative retelling of the big story through a poem. The Father and the Son paint the world in glorious colour, only for The Poisoned Pool to appear and suck all the colour out of the world. The Son is sent to earth and proceeds to remove the effects of the pool by drinking every last drop of poison, allowing colour to re-enter the world. The refrain that features throughout:

He splashed out with the richest rainbow:
Painting indigo for some get up and go.
He drew red for the helpless, yellow for the hopeless
Blue for the worried, green for the weary.
Violet for the lonely, orange for the sad.
The full spectrum soared and made people glad.
The Son of the Father, plus Helper made one
With so much colour; so much fun,
So many shades and so many sheens,
He brought so much beauty to so many scenes.

Rob Lacey, *The Poisoned Pool* (laceytheatrecompany.com)

Hope in Verse:

One short sleep past, we wake eternally,
And Death shall be no more; Death, thou shalt die.

John Donne (English poet, 1572–1631)

Hope Quote:

Laughter as liturgy

In the Baroque period the liturgy used to include the *risus paschalis*, the Easter laughter. The Easter homily had to contain a story that made people laugh, so that the church sounded with a joyful laughter. … Is there not something very beautiful and appropriate about laughter becoming a liturgical symbol?

Joseph Cardinal Ratzinger (now Pope Benedict XVI), *Images of Hope: Meditations on Major Feasts* (Ignatius Press 1997)

Question of Hope:

Will Jesus come back to earth again?

Some say that Jesus will come back to earth once his people have established his kingdom here. We need to work to build the kingdom of God on earth, and then Jesus will come to claim his crown and reign as King.

Some say that he'll come back when things on earth are so bad that he decides to intervene dramatically to establish his kingdom. The world will simply decline morally and materially, getting worse and worse until Christ comes to rapture his people, exercise judgment and announce his reign of a new earth.

Some say his return is metaphorical; that we shouldn't expect to see him physically on earth again. Jesus comes again to earth through his Holy Spirit into the lives of individuals who receive him; Jesus comes again into the world through the life of his church; Jesus comes again into the world through political and social transformation.

What is clear from the Bible is that Jesus said that he will come back, and we are to watch for signs of his appearing. We are not to know the details of how and when, but we are to be watchful and waiting. That is, we need to live lives of urgent expectation that he will return – soon. When he does, no one will miss it – he'll not come as a baby, but as a King. That's the nature of hope: Living now in light of what we know will come, but hasn't happened... yet!

Rev. Dr. Anna Robbins
Acting Principal,
London School of Theology

2 ONE HOPE ON A HILL

Comment: "It is only after Christ's resurrection that … resurrection is possible. The Old Testament is correct that until that event, human beings are bound for Sheol. After that they are asleep in Sheol until resurrection day, but being in Sheol can be reframed as being with Christ, because while we sleep through those years, Christ protects us and keeps us safe for that final day when we will awake and be raised."

John Goldingay, "Eschatology in Isaiah" in Stephen Holmes & Russell Rook (eds.), *What Are We Waiting For?* (Paternoster Press, Milton Keynes, 2008)

space for notes

wishful thinking nor theological speculation. It is secured by Jesus, the first to rise from among the dead.

In the time we have left, we will reflect on four implications of the resurrection for our own future.

The future is physical

The resurrection was a physical event. At times, the church has almost played down this side of the story. When we think of eternity we tend to emphasise soul and spirit at the expense of physical. The gospel writers, however, go to great lengths to establish the physicality of the risen Jesus. He eats and drinks, allows Thomas to touch his scars and is, in most part, recognisable. While his wounds have healed they remain visible as a sign of his glory. The marks of a humiliating execution have been beautified by God's Spirit.

Attempts to turn Jesus into a ghost, angel or spiritual will-o'-the-wisp are a result of ignorance of the gospel. This type of dualism, where spirituality is put above physicality, damages both the church and the creation. As with Christ, so too with his disciples. We also receive a new body at the resurrection.

The resurrection story challenges us to think more about our physical bodies and the physical world. Our physical bodies are part of God's plan and purpose for creation. We should care for and enjoy them. Diet, health care, fitness, fashion, sexuality and many more issues must find their way into our theology and discipleship. Likewise, the environment, urban planning, rural affairs and other topics relating to the physical world must play a role in the life and mission of the church. We will return to this in the next section when we consider the implications of Christ's resurrection for the physical world.

The future is memorable

It is important to note that not only Jesus' body but his life as a whole is resurrected. Jesus is reacquainted with friends, picks up his preaching where he left off and repeats miracles. God resurrects the whole person – body, mind, soul and history.

God will transform everything we are and redeem everything we have experienced. Jesus' scars show that his crucifixion has not been reversed by his resurrection. The events of Calvary cannot be undone, but they can be redeemed. The resurrection cannot alter past events, but it can redeem them. Hence, the baggage that weighs us down in this world will be a testimony to the power of Christ's resurrection in the next world. We shall see that nothing is beyond the power of God's healing, redeeming and life-giving Spirit.

THE BIG STORY
ONE
GOD
PEOPLE
HOPE
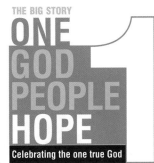
Celebrating the one true God

Hope in Verse:

Jesus reigns

Jesus shall reign where'er the Sun
Does his successive journeys run;
His Kingdom stretch from shore to shore,
Till moons shall wax and wane no more
Isaac Watts (1674–1748), the father of English hymnody

Hope Quote:

Life after death

The Christian religion… is not concerned to make much ado about life after death in general but it must bring out its quite specific gospel that life is in Christ.
Carol Zaleski, The Life of the World to Come: Near-Death Experience and Christian Hope (Oxford University Press 1996)

Story of Hope:

Lost, found and eternally redeemed

The Christian faith maintains that God redeems and resurrects our whole life, our history if you will. A few months ago, Richard passed away. Through his family's grief, the gospel promises redemption. As hard as it may sound, some may occur in the here and now. Susan, Richard's wife, may remarry, and find new love and life with another. Her new husband may provide their kids with a wonderful step-dad, one who in some provisional manner might make up for the absence of their birth father. And yet, the resurrection of Christ promises more than this. Somehow, in eternity God will redeem all that this family has gone through. In their eternal future together as a family, God will restore all that has been lost in time, only this time death will not threaten or harm them.

Questions of Hope:

Hope of heaven

For me, heaven will be catch-up time. I love this life, so other than healing my blindness I'm not necessarily looking for anything radically different. I'd just like to try it all over again, with the added benefit of 20/20 vision.

First will come the car. The celestial transport system may well be excellent, but I shall be tearing up the heavenly tarmac in my own set of wheels. Then I'll open a bookshop. I can't wait to be able to pick up any book, anytime, anywhere and just read it, without the hassle of getting it put into an accessible format. And not forgetting the scenery! At last I won't have to make do with other people's valiant but hopelessly inadequate descriptions of mountain ranges; I will finally be able to enjoy them for myself.

Before you conclude that I must be the ultimate materialist, some reassurance. My first real surge of joy at the prospect of heaven came when I learnt these words, from an old and familiar chorus: "When I stand in glory, I will see his face."

These are words full of wonder for anyone who has spent a lifetime following Jesus, but for me, a deeper wonder. When I stand in glory, I will see his face. After years of knowing and loving his voice, I will get a whole new revelation of him. Whenever the healing from blindness comes, I can ask nothing better than that his face should be the first thing I see.

Lyndall Bywater
24-7/SA Prayer Network Coordinator,
The Salvation Army

2 ONE HOPE ON A HILL

According to Christian eschatology, everything we achieve that is true, good and beautiful in God's eyes lives on in eternity. What we do and who we are is not lost, but is perfected in the next world. Take the relationships we enjoy here and now. Will they continue in the new creation? Theologians answer this question in different ways. If nothing good gets lost in heaven then we can expect our relationships to be present and perfected in the new creation. Furthermore, if God resurrects our lives and not just our physical bodies then relationships which are intrinsic to our identity – husbands and wives, parents and children, friends, loved ones, etc. – must surely have some place in our eternal future.

Theologians are often nervous about assigning details to the relationships we will share in the new creation. What we can say is that we will experience a greater quality and quantity of relationships than we do at present. Where we now enjoy a limited number of relationships, and all of them are restricted by sinfulness, in the new creation we will have perfect relationships with God, humanity and creation. While it is possible to suggest that friends, family and loved ones will have some role to play in this world, it is impossible to say exactly how these and other relationships will pan out in eternity.

The future is hopeful

Jesus' resurrection is not the end of hope but the beginning. By redeeming our past God grants us an eternal future. Christian accounts of the new creation often fail to do justice to this future, sometimes making the afterlife appear undesirable. Many people find the prospect of endless clouds with everlasting harp recitals and unending choir practice wholly unattractive.

There appears to be an absence of hope in many visions of the afterlife. If there is nothing left to hope for after our resurrection, then surely eternal life is hardly worth having. If Christ's resurrection is the antidote for human hopelessness, then surely our own resurrection marks the beginning of a new and eternal hopefulness. Our hope does not result from sin or dissatisfaction, for in this world sin has died and humanity is satisfied. Our hope will be fulfilled in the new creation and extended by God's infinite goodness and love. We will enjoy God's life with one another for ever. We literally have eternity to look forward to.

The future's been and is coming

Jesus' resurrection marks the dawn of the last days – the time during which God's plans will be realised. Some people are prepared to say that the resurrection of Christ is the very end of the world as we know it. In his resurrection we witness the final outcome of God's creation and of human history. Life, the gospel assures us, doesn't end in death – but in resurrection. We don't finish our

Hope in Verse:

A marvellous healing

He ran

through the unfamiliar sunlight,

drinking it in,

experiencing it all at once

the thousand and one feelings

that for so long had been denied him.

It was a marvellous healing;

to be so totally restored,

made whole,

rebuilt.

It had just surprised him,

a little,

that he had to die

to receive it.

Gerard Kelly, *Spoken Worship* (Zondervan 2007)

Stories of Hope:

Bored to death in heaven

In chapter ten of his wonderfully inventive book *A History of the World in 10½ Chapters*, Julian Barnes tells the story of a man who wakes to find himself in heaven. He discovers that he is able to satiate every human desire and appetite instantaneously, so he enjoys his favourite food at every meal. He takes up golf and becomes so good that he can complete a round in 18 shots. After a time he goes to the administration and asks to die. He finds out that everyone asks to die eventually, so boring does life become when everything is immediate and there is nothing to hope for. Barnes is obviously looking for a new kind of eternal life. The kind which is beyond anything so far imagined and not simply an endless repetition of the present.

Richard Bauckham, commenting on the book, says, "Hope in this world has to do with dissatisfaction with the present. That is why in this world it's better to travel hopefully than

to arrive. Arriving is always disappointing because we can always envisage something better. Nothing in this world is ever wholly satisfying.

"But life with God in eternity will be fully satisfying. It will be much better to have arrived than to be still travelling. In particular the beatific vision is what we are made for and it entirely fulfils our nature. This is the traditional view and I think objections to it arise from the perspective of the Barnes' story – imagining eternal life as much like the present except that opportunities for the sort of thing we enjoy in this life will be endless. Crucially God is missing from that story."

The Christian doctrine of Christ's resurrection makes it clear that we have everything left to hope for.

days in a grave, we are resurrected to eternal life. The world doesn't die, it gives way to a new heaven and a new earth.

Whether the Easter event was the end of the world or a sign of the end, we can all agree that it was the weekend that changed the world for ever. Questions about God's involvement in the here and now have been answered. There is encouragement for those who mourn and grieve. And vindication for those who believed that life could overcome death. Eternal hope is alive and available through the risen Christ, whose life and reign will never end. Our stories end in resurrection, not death. Through Jesus, the eternally happy ending of God's big story becomes the promised end of our lives.

2.3
Waking the dead

The church, the community founded by the risen Jesus and filled with his spirit, is the new humanity. As God's people, our hope extends beyond the grave into eternal life. We have seen how the big story ends, so we should be the most hopeful people on earth. While others foresee only doom for the world, we can stand tall and shout for all to hear that there is good news. We must protest in the power of the resurrection against sickness and disease, deprived communities, broken relationships and hopeless individuals. We know that God has conquered death by the power of Jesus' resurrection.

All human beings know that life is impossible without hope, but we, unlike many, have an unending supply of hope in the risen Jesus. By guiding people to the eternal life-giver, we become life-savers. Our job is to tell the world that Jesus was raised from the dead, to involve ourselves in community regeneration, to offer opportunities to the excluded, to care for the rejected, to provide justice for the hard-done-by and, above all, to outline and live out the gospel's compelling vision for a renewed creation. We are called to give the kiss of resurrection life to the world in which we live.

On this theme, we can learn a lot from the history of God's people. Time and again the church has used the power of the resurrection to defy the curse of death, and her opponents struggle to contest this. While some would be happy to eject the church from public life, most foresee disaster down this road. The detrimental impact on schools, health care, social services, the developing world and much more besides is unthinkable. What's more, while God's people could down tools today the transformative influence of our forebears cannot be

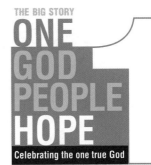
THE BIG STORY

ONE
GOD
PEOPLE
HOPE
1
Celebrating the one true God

Story of Hope:

Sunday's coming

He started his sermon real softly by saying, 'It was Friday; it was Friday and my Jesus was dead on the tree. But that was Friday, and Sunday's comin'!' One of the Deacons yelled, 'Preach, brother, preach!' It was all the encouragement he needed. He came on louder as he said, 'It was Friday and Mary was cryin' her eyes out. The disciples were runnin' in every direction, like sheep without a shepherd, but that was Friday, and Sunday's comin'!'

The preacher kept going. He picked up the volume still more… He kept on working that one phrase for… an hour and a half. Over and over he came at us, 'It's Friday, but Sunday's comin'!' … He had me and everybody else so worked up that I don't think any of us could have stood it much longer. At the end of his message he just yelled at the top of his lungs, 'It's FRIDAY!' and all 500 of us in that church yelled back with one accord, 'SUNDAY'S COMIN'!'

Tony Campolo, *It's Friday, but Sunday's Comin'* (Paternoster 1985), 124–126

Hope Note:

Noting hope

There are many examples of famous non-Christians noting the power of hope found in the biblical story. New York-based writer and lecturer Douglas Rushkoff, for example, recently launched a comic book series called *Testament* that intertwines biblical narrative and fiction within a futuristic framework. He comments on the negative reaction he has received from religious fundamentalists who didn't want their story messed with:

"Yet these so-called men of God and the phony politicians they support are the very forces the Bible was written to warn us about! These Scripture-thumping mind controllers are the last ones who want us to connect with the real power in these myths. I'm not bashing the Bible at all. I'm actually attempting to restore its integrity as perhaps the most transcendent narrative ever developed. If just a few people would truly read these stories, we wouldn't be led around like zombies any more. We couldn't. It'd be like returning to normal after an intense psychedelic trip; it's just too late to go back."

Hope Note:

One people, one hope

In an article in *The Guardian* (12 September 2005) subtitled 'We atheists have to accept that most believers are better human beings', longtime Labour Party politician Roy Hattersley writes: "Good works, John Wesley insisted, are no guarantee of a place in heaven. But they are most likely to be performed by people who believe that heaven exists.

"The correlation is so clear that it is impossible to doubt that faith and charity go hand in hand. The close relationship may have something to do with the belief that we are all God's children… . Whatever the reason, believers answer the call."

http://www.guardian.co.uk/comment/story/0,3604,1567604,00.html

Keys – a different way to pray

Search in your pocket or handbag for your set of keys and hold them in one hand. (If you don't have your keys with you, then picture them in your mind.) Much as members of the Roman Catholic Church use rosary beads as a wonderfully creative aid to prayer, we're going to use keys as a way of praying through the various locations in which we are evidence of Christ's resurrection, the bearers of his Spirit and the couriers of his good news.

Everyone's set of keys is different, but most include keys for a house and a vehicle, and have a key fob or something that identifies the set of keys.

Using the keys, pray for each location that they represent. For example,

- HOUSE KEY: spend time praying for your home, your family, your neighbours, the street where you live.
- CAR KEY: pray for the key places you travel to.
- KEY FOB: this represents you. Maybe there are places and people you dream of reaching with the good news of resurrection, but so far these dreams have remained unrealised. Spend time praying for the places that are on your heart.

undone. For centuries the church has testified to the resurrection by refusing to allow the world to go to the dogs and by insisting upon a better future.

We remain charged and commissioned to defy death. Not to deny death's existence, but to make it clear that death is not the end of God's story. In the same way that the women rushed to the tomb to attend to Jesus' dead body, we must rush to the parts of our communities where death has taken hold and proclaim with boldness that it need not end this way. For we, God's people, are the evidence of Christ's resurrection, the bearers of the Holy Spirit and couriers of the good news.

Conclusion
Living in the long good Saturday

Before we conclude, let's remind ourselves of the story so far…

The king surprising

- THE KING PROMISING: Isaiah's poetry and prophecy provide exiled Israel with the hope of a brand new day. God has not broken his promise and his people are not beyond saving. In Jesus, God provides a new king to save the day.

- THE KING ARRIVING: When God's chosen one finally arrives, he is not what many expect. He looks more like a servant than a king. In Jesus, the servant king, we discover authentic royalty and genuine deity.

- THE KING DYING: Having promised us an eternal kingdom, the king of creation dies. This is not God's defeat but his victory. Jesus serves us by confronting death on our behalf.

The king rising

- HE'S ALIVE: Having raised Jesus from the dead, God has defeated death once and for all and proved that nothing can undermine his life-giving power. The resurrected Jesus is available to us. He is ready, willing and able to be part of our story.

- THE FUTURE'S BRIGHT: The resurrection is not only the end of Jesus' story on earth but the happy ending of all creation. Resurrection also marks the end of our story as God's people since now we can share in his death and resurrection and receive his eternal life.

Certain Rumour **by Russell Rook**
Join Cleopas and the disciple with no name as they wander down the Emmaus Road with the risen Jesus. This book retells the big story of the Bible from the vantage point of the resurrection, and proves that it is a short walk to hope.

Hope Note:

The when of God's kingdom

The three main positions into which the hope of the kingdom falls have been helpfully outlined by I. Howard Marshall, Emeritus Professor of New Testament Exegesis at Aberdeen University.

- REALISED ESCHATOLOGY, the view associated with the influential British theologian Charles Harold Dodd (1884–1973), sees the kingdom as already present through Jesus.

- THOROUGHGOING ESCHATOLOGY, the contribution of German theologians Johannes Weiss (1863–1914) and Albert Schweitzer (1875–1965), maintains that the kingdom will only occur in the future when God brings all things to their culmination.

- SELF-REALIZING ESCHATOLOGY, espoused by many theologians, sees the arrival of the kingdom as a process in which the kingdom has come but is still to come.

Hope Quote:

Power now, but not fully

We truly experience the powers of the new age here and now, but we do not experience them to the full; we are truly redeemed from sin, but we have not fully escaped from it. ... What is going on is that the new life is already at work within us, but it is within our frail, corruptible bodies that this work of renewal is secretly going on. We are always bearing in the body the dying of Jesus that the life of Jesus may also be visible in our corruptible bodies.

Howard Marshall, "Eschatology in the New Testament," *What Are We Waiting For?*

One Hope DVD course
A six-session DVD resource that brings expert input, provocative panel discussions and inspiring stories into small groups. Covering the themes of the Spring Harvest week, One Hope is a great opportunity to consolidate learning and share Spring Harvest back home.

2 ONE HOPE
ON A HILL

• WAKING THE DEAD: BY THE POWER OF THE HOLY SPIRIT, CHRIST'S RESURRECTION IS ALREADY MAKING US INTO NEW CREATIONS. WE ARE CALLED TO CARRY THE GOOD NEWS OF CREATION'S FUTURE TO THE WORLD.

Final thoughts

So where do we leave this chapter in the big story? Did the kingdom come with the resurrection of Jesus, or are we still waiting? The answer is probably 'Yes'. The kingdom came when Jesus fulfilled the prophecies about him written in Isaiah. God has won his cosmic battle with death. The coronation of Jesus has happened in time and space, and his resurrection means he can never be deposed. On the other hand, sin and death are still around and we know that the outworking of the Easter miracle is far from complete. A new day has dawned, but much remains to be done.

We are living in the now and not yet of God's kingdom, experiencing a tension that is always hopeful if rarely easy. The German theologian Oscar Cullman used to call it the theological equivalent of living between D-Day and VJ-Day. Although the allied forces effectively won World War II on 6 June 1944, it was not until 2 September 1945 that the enemy finally surrendered and the victory was finally and fully secured. As the community of the resurrected Christ (the servant king of Israel and the creator of the world) we live in the assurance that the cosmic battle between life and death has been won by life and our eternal future is safe. However, we await the outworking of this victory. Skirmishes continue between life and death, and there is much work to be done before the kingdom is fully realised.

For now, we are left to live in the long good Saturday. This is different to the dark Saturday that followed the crucifixion. Living after the resurrection, we know that Jesus is alive and that the future of the church and his world are safe in him.

Recommended Reading

A Shorter Read

What Are We Waiting For? ed. Stephen R. Holmes and Russell Rook (Paternoster Press 2008)

Leading theologians and Christian thinkers discuss the issue of hope as it relates to theology, the Bible, the church and culture. The essays aim to provide a short and informative read.

"New Testament Eschatology" by Howard Marshall

Marshall's guide to New Testament eschatology provides a great survey of how the church has interpreted Christ's hope in history.

A Longer Read

The Wondrous Cross: Atonement and Penal Substitution in the Bible and History by Stephen R. Holmes (Paternoster Press 2007)

Offers an accessible and authoritative account of the way the saving work of Jesus is presented in the Bible, and has been understood throughout Christian history. In particular, the book offers background to the current debates about penal substitutionary atonement by looking at that idea in biblical and historical perspectives.

A Deeper Read

Surprised by Hope by Tom Wright (SPCK 2007)

One of the foremost scholars of our day unpacks the hope that the gospel brings to the world.

BOOK OF THE DAY

A Book for all the Family

The Poisoned Pool by Rob Lacey

This wonderful illustrated book tells the story of creation, the fall and redemption in a simple and memorable way, using the metaphor of colour for the hope that Jesus brings into, and then restores to, the world. Only available through the Lacey Theatre Company website http://laceytheatrecompany.com/

Resources for churches

Hope with a Passion by Krish and Miriam Kandiah (Spring Harvest 2008)

The latest Spring Harvest workbook explores Christ's experience of crucifixion and resurrection. Explore the significance of the cross and resurrection for our lives, hopes and relationships. Track this theme of hope through the Bible and discover how the story of the Passion is an antidote to hopelessness, has answers to life´s big questions and is an anticipation of heaven.

Hope in the garden
Introduction

Yesterday we explored the Easter story as the defining moment in Christian hope. Today we flip back to the beginning of the big story in search of the hope of creation, which we shall explore from three perspectives.

1. ISAIAH: We will find that the story of creation brings hope to people in pain.

2. THE NEW TESTAMENT: In coming to terms with Christ's hope, the early church found a vision for creation.

3. THE CHURCH: In our own context, concerns regarding the future of the planet are high on the public agenda. How does the Christian notion of hope inform the church's position?

THE BIG STORY
ONE
GOD
PEOPLE
HOPE
Celebrating the one true God
1

Teaching Block 1:

Hope of Creation

In Teaching Block 1 we will explore...

- The hopefulness of God's presence in creation.
- The hopefulness of God's purposes and plans before the creation of the earth.
- The hopefulness of creation after the fall and to the ends of the earth.

Teaching Block 2:

Hope of New Creation

In Teaching Block 2 we will reflect upon...

- Ways in which God achieves his plans for creation.
- Ways in which the Bible depicts the end of the earth.
- Ways in which the church can respond to today's ecological crisis.

Teaching Block 1:

"The time will surely come when everything in your palace, and all that your fathers have stored up until this day, will be carried off to Babylon. Nothing will be left, says the LORD. And some of your descendants, your own flesh and blood who will be born to you, will be taken away, and they will become eunuchs in the palace of the king of Babylon."

Isaiah 39:6–7

Comfort, comfort my people, says your God. Speak tenderly to Jerusalem, and proclaim to her that her hard service has been completed, that her sins have been paid for, that she has received from the LORD's hand double for all her sins.

Isaiah 40:1–2

Comment: "Paul Hanson calls Isaiah's heavenly council 'the nerve center of the universe.'"

Paul D. Hanson, *Isaiah 40–66*
(Interpretation Bible Commentaries)
(Westminster/John Knox Press, 1995), 18

Hope of creation

1.1
Here endeth the lesson

What a difference a chapter makes. Between the terrifying warning of Isaiah 39 and the tender warmth of Isaiah 40 was a painfully long period during which a large proportion of Israel's finest citizens were bundled off to Babylon to serve a foreign king. Jerusalem lay in ruins and the temple was a pile of rubble. More than a century was to pass before the exiles returned to Jerusalem and the city returned to God's people.

Isaiah 40 is Israel's alarm call, announcing the beginning of a new day. It must have sounded like a great hymn, an oratorio of hope proclaiming an end to the excruciating and seemingly irrevocable breakdown in the relationship between Israel and God. "Comfort, comfort," the prophet sings, intoning the word Israel most desperately wants to hear twice so it isn't missed.

The setting, a kind of court room, occurs elsewhere in Isaiah. The poetry describes heaven's high council, the group through whom God governs the universe. The many heavenly voices are all used by God to speak to his people, on this occasion to discuss Israel's pleas and accusations.

Jerusalem's fall and the kidnapping of Israel's leaders raised big questions. Having been promised so much, Israel feels rejected. Has God become tired of her iniquities? Is it possible God has divorced her? Could he have sold Israel to the Babylonian gods? Questions abound, but answers seem hard to come by.

Isaiah 40 is God's response to his people's doubting, shouting, questioning and blaspheming. Take note, he allows their complaints to be heard in his highest court. We may resist pressing God with our most honest questions but the Bible encourages us to do this. In Isaiah this exchange marks the start of a new day

THE BIG STORY
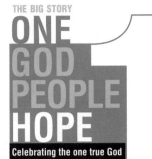
ONE
GOD
PEOPLE
HOPE
Celebrating the one true God
1

Hope Note:

The exile and identity

The exile refers to a period between 587 and 538 BC, when the southern kingdom of Judah had collapsed under the attacks of the Babylonians and a good part of the Judean population was exiled to the land of Babylonia.

In 587, King Nebuchadnezzar laid siege to Jerusalem, destroying and plundering the city and taking many of its residents captive; the deportations targeted officials, military leaders, religious leaders and other vital figures.

During their struggles as exiles in a foreign land, the Israelites were able to maintain their faith in the one true God. Since they could no longer worship Yahweh through animal sacrifice at the temple, they established gatherings (later known as synagogues) for prayer and the study of Torah.

At this point in history they became designated 'Jews'. Cyrus the Great of Persia conquered Babylonia in 538 BC, and after many years of trial the Jews were restored their freedom. Many returned to the homeland, where they awaited the building of the second temple.

Stories of Hope:

African mass silence

Every so often, hope bursts into our lives in the most extraordinary way. In the season of Lent the Roman Catholic church enters a period of austerity: colourful vestments are replaced by sombre purple; the buildings remain undecorated by flowers or garlands; musical instruments are withdrawn from worship; the mood is quiet and contemplative.

As Holy Week dawns and the Passion of the Christ is recalled, the atmosphere darkens and the silence deepens. There is a particular moment in the Easter liturgy when the overwhelming joy of the Lord's resurrection breaks out in a wonderful cacophony as the celebrant of the Eucharist intones the opening words of the Gloria: *Gloria in excelsis Deo*. The organ (if there is one) and any other instruments play and all the bells of the church are rung.

Two years ago Brian Horne, a lecturer in Christian Doctrine at King's College London, was in South Africa, worshipping in a large working-class parish in Pretoria during the season of Lent. He recalls how, on Holy Saturday, he entered the silence and darkness of the church, still contemplating Christ's descent into hell, to await the resurrection and the coming of the light and music of Easter.

The Eucharist began and the Gloria was intoned, he says, but instead of the expected organs and bells, drums began beating: at first softly, then more and more loudly.

"It was as though the earth was being split open by the noise of the Lord's triumphant return from the grave," he says. "The Gloria which followed, sung in typical African full-throated style, was also a kind of shout of triumph – all to the astonishing sound of African drums."

as God, in a gracious response to outrageous allegations, provides strength for today and hope for tomorrow.

> Who has measured the waters in the hollow of his hand, or with the breadth of his hand marked off the heavens? Who has held the dust of the earth in a basket, or weighed the mountains on the scales and hills in a balance? Who has understood the mind of the LORD, or instructed him as his counsellor? Whom did the LORD consult to enlighten him, and who taught him the right way? Who was it that taught him knowledge or showed him the path of understanding?
>
> Isaiah 40:12–14

Comment: "The prophet employs a series of rhetorical questions intended to bring the reader to the point of saying that Yahweh is the sole creator."

John N. Oswalt, *Isaiah (The NIV Application Commentary)* (Zondervan, 2003), 446

> Do you not know? Have you not heard? The LORD is the everlasting God, the Creator of the ends of the earth.
>
> Isaiah 40:28

1.2
In the beginning, hope...

The legal proceedings get under way with heaven's councillors cross-examining Israel. Their many questions can be summarised as 'Who made the heavens and the earth?' This is not an attempt to change the subject but rather to give Israel new hope. For this, she must return to the beginning of the big story.

Hope begins in creation. This is not to say that creation is hopeful in and of itself, but rather that God made the world hopeful. By rephrasing the same question over and over again, heaven's councillors challenge Israel to look beyond her immediate predicament and find her answers in God. *Who* has measured the waters? *Who* held the dust of the earth? *Who* created the heavens? *Who* calls out every star by name? The answer is simple and it is always the same, God did. Why? Because of his high hopes for creation and even higher hopes for people.

But what about the fall, how did that affect God's hope for creation? For some, the story of hope begins after the fall. Sin has thrown the universe into crisis, and hope is the possibility that things might turn out right after all. Hope is a redemptive or punitive measure; hope makes bad things go away; hope mends creation. While this view is undoubtedly correct, it doesn't paint the whole picture.

Isaiah tells us that God had hopes for creation before the fall. He made the world to be dynamic, not static. He purposely made it to bring himself glory. So creation is more a project than an object. The Bible says God made the world good and planned to perfect it. This surprises people who assume the Garden of Eden was made perfect. When God surveys his creation in Genesis chapter one, he does not pronounce it 'perfect' but 'good'.

The possibility of sin and death is often cited in support of this view. The garden could not have been perfect if sin and death were possible, and we know they were because Adam and Eve sinned and died. This doesn't mean they *had* to sin. God clearly made them to enjoy eternal life but the possibility that they might misuse their free will made this unhappy ending possible from the beginning.

Chesterton and the Teletubbies

Imogen loves watching the Teletubbies on television. She is only 18 months old, but like all well-behaved and godly children is instantly silenced by four large cuddly creatures of limited vocabulary.

Imogen doesn't really understand the programme and happily watches the same episode over and over again. However it has taught her to say 'gen', her first word. Gen is toddlerish for again, and Imogen is more than happy to wander round the house saying 'gen' to anything and everything. When she is fed, gen. When she's tickled, gen. When she is read a story, gen.

In his book *Orthodoxy*, G.K. Chesterton paints a wonderful picture of a God so carried away with the beauty of his creation that he wanders around saying the equivalent of 'gen'. Gen to the sunrise every new morning, gen to snow drops every spring, gen to the snows of winter each year, gen to the high tide every evening, gen to our every breath, gen every time we please him, gen every time we make him smile.

He writes: "It may not be automatic necessity that makes all daisies alike; it may be that God makes every daisy separately, but has never got tired of making them. It may be that He has the eternal appetite of infancy; for we have sinned and grown old, and our Father is younger than we."

A message of hope for the dying?

'Where can I go from your spirit? Or where can I flee from your presence? If I ascend to heaven you are there…

In your book were written all the days that were formed for me…

Lead me in the way everlasting'. (Psalm 139 NRSV)

Dying is the gateway to the new, the beginning of eternal life, faith fulfilled. For the Lord's people, it is wonderful and exciting … in theory.

In practice it can be messy: painful, even agony, with physical, emotional or spiritual distress. A mother watches her dying child; a divorcee could find relationships tangled; pain relief stops working; sins and things undone resurface and attack a soul's peace.

A dying person, in a safe appropriate environment, needs time with God, to ask for and receive forgiveness, perhaps anointing with oil, for the Holy Spirit's peace to indwell. Bible readings such as Psalm 23, 121, 139, Revelation 21, John 14, and Christian music either sung or played, telling the old old story of God's eternal love. A wooden cross, gently placed onto a dying palm, without the need of words. Compassion, love and just being there are physical ways of embodying hope, speaking volumes to the dying and to those who love them.

The dying need both our love and assurance that Jesus Christ did die on the cross for us, he calls us by our names, he will never abandon us at our time of ultimate need.

Mia Hilborn
Hospitaller and Head of Chaplaincy,
Guy's and St Thomas' NHS Foundation Trust

3 ONE HOPE IN THE GARDEN

space for notes

Comment "*Tōbh*, the Hebrew word for good, has a wide range of meanings. The least common is 'morally good'. Much more common are: 'aesthetic beauty' or 'fit for purpose'. The meaning 'fit for purpose' seems to be the most appropriate one in Genesis 1. God's creation was 'good' in that it was ideally fit for his purposes."

Ernest Lucas, vice-principal and tutor in biblical studies at Bristol Baptist College

Comment: "It is never enough for Isaiah for God's hope to simply address the balance. God's hope is for the whole of creation to find him. As Basil of Caesarea writes, 'All things that exist, then, come from him…. Through him things endure over time and are maintained, for he created all things and gives to each what is needed for its well-being. Therefore all things are oriented to him, looking with irresistible longing and inexpressive desire to the Creator and Sustainer of life.'"

Basil of Caesarea, cited in Robert Louis Wilken (ed. trans.), *Isaiah: Interpreted by Early Christian and Medieval Commentators* (Eerdmans, 2007)

A voice says, "Cry out." And I said, "What shall I cry?" "All men are like grass, and all their glory is like the flowers of the field. The grass withers and the flowers fall, because the breath of the LORD blows on them. Surely the people are grass. The grass withers and the flowers fall, but the word of our God stands for ever."

Isaiah 40:6–8

One of the chief differences between this world and the next world is the possibility and presence of sin and death in this world. They were possible before the fall, and they are present after the fall. In the next world they will be impossible, having been defeated by Christ's death and resurrection. Sin and death will be no more and creation will be perfected. Until then, God's creation project remains a work in progress.

Isaiah reminded Israel that creation was an exercise in divine hopefulness and that as God's chosen people they were an essential part of God's hope for creation. Despite their circumstances, Isaiah said, they should hope beyond hope. He said God's people should raise their expectations of what God might do and hope harder than ever before. Isaiah stretches the imagination of God's people by calling on them to visualise the construction of a superhighway. Not a motorway back to Jerusalem, out of exile, but a route along which God would travel to be with his people.

The church often encourages conservatism. Don't dream too big, you'll only be disappointed, it says. Don't aim too high, you'll only miss. But Isaiah says our problem is not that we hope too much, but that we hope too little and so miss out on the infinite hopefulness of God.

In recent decades, many churches have limited themselves to the hope that more people might come to their services and events. This hope has been largely frustrated. What would happen if we replaced this limited hope with unlimited hope? If we applied God's eternal hope to the pains and problems outside the church? In the West, the time has come to hope for something more than larger congregations. It is time for such extreme hopefulness that Christ's presence enters the towns and communities in which we live.

1.3
Painting the picture, perfect

As part of his creation project, God made partners to work alongside him. His partners, mankind, were central to the completion of his creation. Without us it couldn't be made perfect. Our wilful disregard for this privileged position derailed God's plan. Having introduced sin to the world we now suffer its consequences. We have become like grass, our days are numbered and our glories passing.

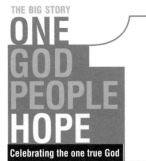

Stories of Hope:

Saving lives

Beachy Head in East Sussex is far better-known than most cliff-tops – achieving its fame through being a notorious suicide spot, the BBC reports.

A dramatic fall in the number of deaths there in 2006 has been credited in part to the dedicated work of the Beachy Head Chaplaincy Team (BHCT), whose members carry out evening patrols, or respond to call-outs and run an aftercare service.

"Some people get to a place where they can see no answer other than to end their lives," Pastor Ross Hardy told the BBC. "There's a lot more pressure on people nowadays, for example a husband and wife having to work all hours to pay the bills and the mortgage."

The Maritime and Coastguard Agency said BHCT had developed a "proven and effective role [in] managing the Beachy Head situation."

The team were honoured in 2006 with the Spring Harvest Faithworks Community Innovation Award for Developing Projects.

"Our desire as always is to put a stop to these suicides at Beachy Head," Ross said.

http://news.bbc.co.uk/1/hi/england/
southern_counties/6197229.stm

Hope Quote:

Aimlessness

When something is not fulfilling its potential and purpose; that is frustration. Nature has been subjected to this state of frustration. There is just about nowhere you can look where nature is fulfilling its true purpose. What is that purpose? To glorify God and to support human beings. Nature manifestly does not fulfil that God-ordained design in its fallen state.

Mark Stibbe, *On the Future of Creation*

Hope Quote:

Mending creation

Man is born broken. He lives by mending. The grace of God is the glue.

Eugene O'Neill (1888–1953), Nobel prize winning American playwright

Stories of Hope:

Atonement

In the novel *Atonement*, Ian McEwan tells the compelling stories of a group of characters who are all trying to pay for their sins or right the wrongs that have been done to them. What becomes clear is that atonement, by our efforts at least, is an impossible goal. In the end, it takes a clever author to write forgiveness, healing and justice into the story. The book is a beautiful parable of gospel hope. It takes an all-knowing, all-loving God to make redemption possible. In Jesus, God wrote this into the big story from the start.

3 ONE HOPE
IN THE GARDEN

Do you not know? Have you not heard? Has it not been told you from the beginning? Have you not understood since the earth was founded? He sits enthroned above the circle of the earth, and its people are like grasshoppers. He stretches out the heavens like a canopy, and spreads them out like a tent to live in. He brings princes to naught and reduces the rulers of this world to nothing. No sooner are they planted, no sooner are they sown, no sooner do they take root in the ground, than he blows on them and they wither, and a whirlwind sweeps them away like chaff.

Isaiah 40:21–24

"To whom will you compare me? Or who is my equal?" says the Holy One. Lift your eyes and look to the heavens: Who created all these? He who brings out the starry host one by one, and calls them each by name. Because of his great power and mighty strength, not one of them is missing.

Isaiah 40:25–26

He who was seated on the throne said, "I am making everything new!"

Revelation 21:5

In the fifteenth year of the reign of Tiberius Caesar…, the word of God came to John son of Zechariah in the desert…. As is written in the book of the words of Isaiah the prophet: "A voice of one calling in the desert, 'Prepare the way for the Lord, make straight paths for him. Every valley shall be filled in, every mountain and hill made low. The crooked roads shall become straight, the rough ways smooth. And all mankind will see God's salvation.'"

Luke 3:1–6

Comment: "In the gospels the mission of John the Baptizer, the 'forerunner,' was seen as announced in Isaiah's cry to prepare the way of the Lord (40:3). Many other events in the gospels were regarded as heralded in Isaiah 40–66. These chapters also became the occasion to reflect on the otherness of and transcendence of God, … on the church's universal mission and the consummation of history."

Robert Louis Wilken (ed. trans.),
Isaiah: Interpreted by Early Christian and Medieval Commentators
(Eerdmans, 2007) 226

Scripture is capable of many surprises and here comes another. This time it's not a twist in the plot, but the lack of a twist. When God's partners in creation fall, his hope remains unchanged. There is no 'Plan B'. In the same way that God is everlasting, so are his purposes.

God is using the very creatures responsible for the fall to fulfil his everlasting purpose for creation. While his plan is evidently hopeful, it also appears to be almost impossible. Perfecting creation was hard enough before the fall but now the entire created order is messed up. And we sinful and selfish mortals are expected to implement God's plan for a perfect world. This is inconceivable, unless God can replace our weakness with strength, sin with purity, exhaustion with energy, and mortality with eternity. In some of the most beautiful lines of Isaiah, heaven promises that God will do exactly this.

The message of Isaiah is as relevant and inspiring as ever. The prophet speaks of God's acts of creation in both past and present tenses for God didn't stop hoping for creation on the sixth day. He continues to realise his hopes for the world through the lives of his people. He is at work in every aspect of creation – he stretches out the heavens and brings out the evening stars one by one, he sits enthroned above the earth and rules history from heaven. God desperately wants his people to grasp his continuing commitment to creation. So much so that in Isaiah 40–55 he interrupts the councillors to deliver a message directly.

God's big story does not end with a patched up planet or corrected creation. At the end, he does not declare, I am making everything 'better'. He says, 'I am making everything new!' God's hopes for creation are undiminished by the fall, he is still intent on perfecting the world and using us to do it.

Scripture outlines three ways in which God uses humanity to herald the world's future perfection.

Firstly, God perfects the world through the humanity of Jesus. The highway in Isaiah refers to the coronation procession of the coming king. John the Baptist used this passage to announce the arrival of Jesus, the second Adam, the one who proved that humanity can live up to God's hopes for creation. Jesus is the Son of God, the fulfilment of Israel and the perfection of mankind. Through his Spirit, the risen Jesus makes his perfected humanity available to us. Our lives are now defined by his purity instead of Adam's sin. Our holy day is Sunday, as opposed to the Jewish Saturday, so that rather than celebrate the day on which God rested we celebrate the day on which Jesus was resurrected and began to make all things new.

space for notes

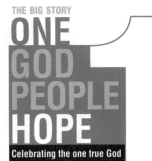

THE BIG STORY

ONE GOD PEOPLE HOPE 1

Celebrating the one true God

Hope Note:

Perfecting perfection

Some theologians have suggested that God created a perfect world and planned to make it more perfect through time. But how can anyone improve upon perfection? In preparing to create a new sculpture, Michelangelo would instruct his assistants to locate a perfect piece of marble. When they found one, Michelangelo would set about carving it into an even more perfect form. In the same way, it has been argued, God could create a perfect world and then, as the one who knows no impossibility, perfect his work further.

Resolving the differences between these arguments is not as difficult as it may first seem. In Hebrew there are two words for 'perfect'. The first (*tam*) indicates perfect innocence. To be *tam* is to be utterly untouched by any impurity. This word might well describe the world's initial innocence upon creation. The second word is *mushlam* and is the root word of shalom. It describes something that has been perfected through a process of sanctification and divine activity. With these words in play we can now argue that God created a perfect (*tam*) world and hoped to further perfect (*mushlam*) it.

Hope in Verse:

See his blood upon the rose

I see his blood upon the rose
And in the stars the glory of his eyes,
His body gleams amid eternal snows,
His tears fall from the skies.

I see his face in every flower;
The thunder and the singing of the birds

Are but his voice – and carven by his power
Rocks are his written words.

All pathways by his feet are worn,
His strong heart stirs the ever-beating sea,
His crown of thorns is twined with every thorn,
His cross is every tree.

Joseph Mary Plunkett (1887–1916), Irish nationalist

Hope Note:

Rembrandt's parable

The artistic process employed by Rembrandt is, according to Nicholas Wolterstorff, the Noah Porter Professor Emeritus of Philosophical Theology at Yale University, a beautiful parable of the way in which God uses our work to complete and perfect his creation.

"A good many of Rembrandt's paintings were initially painted by apprentices in his workshop, Rembrandt then applying the finishing touches. Sometimes… though the

preliminary painting came from the hand of [a] gifted apprentice, and was… very close to being a Rembrandt, it nonetheless fell short in such a way that the master had to do a lot of re-painting in order to make it a Rembrandt. On other occasions, though the apprentice was … very incompetent, he nonetheless somehow produced a painting that required only a bit of tweaking by the master to bring it up to standard."

Nicholas Wolterstorff, "Seeking Justice in Hope",
The Future of Hope (Eerdmans 2004)

space for notes

Secondly, God perfects the world through the humanity of his people. In Isaiah we witness the power of hope in the lives of God's people. At a time when Israel's frailties have been horribly exposed, she lives up to her calling in the most remarkable way. As she exercises hope God meets her and prepares a way for the Messiah. For those of us struggling to hold on to faith, these prophecies speak powerfully. The times we feel most stretched are often the times God uses us most. We are painfully aware of the fractures in Christ's community, but before we give up hope we should remember that it is his broken body that redeems the world.

Thirdly, God perfects the world through the humanity of others. While God has undoubtedly used Israel and the church to activate his hope, he is by no means limited to them. God has used all manner of people to bring about his plan for creation. He used Cyrus, a pagan king, to rescue Israel from exile. The lesson for those of us who tend to limit the means of God's hope is that he uses the whole world to bring about his hope for creation.

2

Teaching Block 2:

Hope of new creation

2.1
Hope in history

> Do you not know? Have you not heard? The LORD is the everlasting God, the Creator of the ends of the earth. He will not grow tired or weary, and his understanding no-one can fathom. He gives strength to the weary and increases the power of the weak. Even youths grow tired and weary, and young men stumble and fall; but those who hope in the LORD will renew their strength. They will soar on wings like eagles; they will run and not grow weary, they will walk and not be faint.
>
> Isaiah 40:28–31

The exile challenged Israel's faith, casting doubt on her belief that God controls history. With the promised land lost and God's people scattered, once confident Israel is a shadow of her former self.

There are striking parallels with the present day. For several hundred years, Christians have accepted a concept of history commonly called modernity and marked by a belief in the power and possibility of history. Advances in thought

Visible hope

God's love expressed in the cross must be made visible in the world through the church.

C. René Padilla, *Mission Between the Times* (Eerdmans 1985)

Strange revolution

Martyn Joseph sings of Jesus coming in a manger and dying on a cross: "What a strange way to start a revolution … and what a strange way to finish your world tour."

We worship the seed that died. The revolution will not be televised. It will not be brought to you by Fox News with commercial interruptions. The revolution will not be televised. It will not be sandwiched between ads to accelerate your life or be all you can be. There will be no re-runs. The revolution will be live. The revolution will be in the streets. The revolution will be cleaning toilets and giving another blanket to Karen. The revolution will not be talking about poverty in hotel banquet rooms.

It will be eating beans and rice with Ms. Sunshine and watching *Back to the Future* with our neighbor Mary. Get ready, friends …

God is preparing us for something really, really – small.

Shane Claiborne in The Simple Way's March 2006 Newsletter
http://www.thesimpleway.org/mailings/Marchnewsletter.pdf

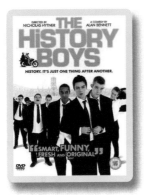

One thing after another

The History Boys is Alan Bennett's moving and hilarious play about a group of grammar school boys trying to get into Oxbridge. It explores how our understanding of history directly impacts the way we live and the choices we make. Rudge, one of the more academically challenged pupils, is asked in his entrance interview, "What is history?" His straightforward reply is: "History is just one damn thing after another!"

Write on the fingers of the left hand below as a way of clarifying five things, values or beliefs you are committed to. For example, creativity might be a defining value of your life, as might honesty or learning. Your five ideals ought to be things that if they were realised would bring hope, imagination and resurrection to those around you.

In his book *Blue Like Jazz*, Donald Miller says that what we believe is what we do. It might be helpful to

examine how you are living out your beliefs. So on the fingers of the right hand below, write your reality – things, values or beliefs that represent how you are actually living out your life right now in contrast with your ideals.

Now look at the things you've written on each hand. Is there a discrepancy between the things you want to define your life and the things you actually do? Are you bringing hope, imagination and resurrection to those around you? If not, what do you need to change?

space for notes

and technology appeared to place history under our control. Greater understanding of the laws of nature, an increasing ability to harness the power of the elements, the rise of democracy and all manner of new and fancy machines has enabled humanity to control its destiny.

The infectious optimism of modernity was soon caught by the church, and the nineteenth century witnessed a surge of eschatological enthusiasm that the twentieth century would mark a new age. The revival of hope had a long-lasting impact, inspiring revival movements, social reforms and the global missions movement to name but a few. While theologies varied in detail, most were soaked in hope. The world was on the verge of something amazing – Jesus' return, a thousand years of Christ's rule prior to Jesus' return, or the consummation of God's kingdom on earth.

Instead we had the bloodiest century in history. So much was promised, but the age birthed two world wars. Human intellectual and technical prowess couldn't prevent third world debt, religious genocides and ecological crisis. Rather than using our knowledge and technology to build God's kingdom, we used them to destroy creation and commit atrocities upon our fellow man. The twentieth century began with hopeful optimism and ended with cynicism and despair. In 1899, many people were excited because they thought God's kingdom was around the corner. In 1999, many people were afraid because they thought the world's computers would crash and cast us into a technological hell.

The disappointments of the last century caused some people to give up on history and certainly influenced the church. As with Israel in exile, opinions are divided. Those who have lost faith in humanity's ability to build God's kingdom view the world's deterioration as necessary, a prelude to God's final intervention. Certain Christians are even prepared to pray for an escalation in conflicts and chaos in the attempt to hasten Christ's return. Other Christians continue to find hope and meaning in human history. For this group the question that arises is, How do we express Christ's hope in the here and now? The question asked by Israel in exile is now ours to answer. To do this we will look to one of the pressing concerns of our own time and place.

2.2
The ends of the earth

Few issues are as pertinent to our discussion of hope as the environment. Conversations about global warming and climate chaos are often apocalyptic in

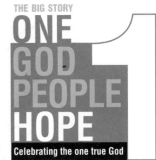

Hope Note:

Millennial theories

The eschatological excitement at the end of the 20th century caused many millennialist theories to take hold in the public imagination. Millennialism is the name given to a range of theories concerning the climax of history. All of these theories result from a popular reading of Revelation regarding Christ reigning for a thousand years prior to the new Jerusalem arriving. There are three main versions of millennialism.

- POSTMILLENNIALISTS argue that Christ will return after this glorious time.

- PREMILLENNIALISTS argue that Christ will return before this glorious time, to rescue the world from darkness.

- AMILLENNIALISTS tend not to read the passage in such a prescriptive way.

David Bebbington writes ('Evangelicals and Eschatology', *What are We Waiting for?*) that the varying positions that Christians have held have invariably affected their expressions of faith and approach to history.

"Postmillennialists were almost always optimistic, believing that Christian teaching will gradually spread over the globe and so transform society for the better.

"Premillennialists tended to be pessimistic, expecting the return of Christ to be imminent and so not seeing the world as worth reforming. Nevertheless they usually held that, because time was short, evangelism was an urgent priority.

"Amillennialists were likely (at least in their own eyes) to be realistic, not having the prospect of a millennium to excite them or a sense that a world without its rightful king was in a state of degeneration.

"Postmillennialism has usually spurred socio-political effort while premillenialism has often discouraged it. Premillennialists have tended to be quietists, deliberately shunning public affairs, or else actively resistant to change, believing that it would operate in the wrong direction."

Hope Quote:

Man the destroyer!

Man is endowed with reason and the power to create, so that he may increase that which has been given him, but until now he has not created, but demolished. The forests are disappearing, the rivers are running dry, the game is exterminated, the climate is spoiled, and the earth becomes poorer and uglier every day.

Anton Chekhov, *Uncle Vanya* (1897)

Hope Quote:

God's judgement

I believe that the various farming crises over the years may well be a judgement of God on the way we are violating creation. The Bible sees judgement not just as an event in the future, a far-off-in-time Day of Judgement, but as a present experience. 'Do not be under any illusion' wrote St Paul 'You cannot make a fool of God. Because, whatever you sow is exactly what you will reap.'

James Jones, Bishop of Liverpool, sermon on Easter morning 2001 http://www.bbc.co.uk/religion/programmes/ sunday_worship/documents/sw20010415s.html

3 ONE HOPE IN THE GARDEN

tone. So how does this fit into God's big story? Is it a fair account of God's hope for creation to see the crisis as a sign of impending destruction?

Christians who expect the eventual destruction of creation usually cite 2 Peter 3:10 and Revelation 21:1. In the first, Peter addresses believers who have given up waiting for Christ's return. If Christ is not coming back then there will be no judgment, so they feel free to contemplate all manner of earthly pleasures.

Peter assures his brothers and sisters that they, along with all creation, will be judged. Some translations of the verse describing God's judgment on creation suggest that the world will be burnt up, but a preferable translation describes creation as being 'laid bare'. This confusion is sometimes compounded by a further misunderstanding. Borrowing a phrase from Isaiah, Peter refers to 'the day of the Lord'. But he doesn't mean 'the final judgment'. Peter is not writing about the end of time, nor is he suggesting that the planet will be destroyed by fire, so this text doesn't support the view that our ecological crisis is the 'hopeful' demise of creation prior to Christ's return. Peter's point is more personal and persistent. He is saying that while only a few of us will see the end of history, we shall all be judged for our part in history.

Writing about creation's final end, the end of the big story, John draws on Isaiah 65:17 to describe the grand finale of God's creation (Rev 21:1). Once again, the wording is key. In describing the new heaven and new earth, John must choose between the two Greek words for *new*. If he uses *neos* it will suggest that the world has been discarded and replaced by a new world. However, John uses *kainos* to indicate that far from being replaced the world will be made new.

The big story does not predict the destruction of the planet. In fact, the Bible foretells the opposite. It speaks of the perfection and renewal of creation. This is important, for the annihilation of creation would cause God to break one of his first promises. Following the flood, God made a covenant with Noah and all the living creatures of the earth and promised to never destroy creation. It is surprising then that so many propose that God reneging on this promise is the end of the big story. Surely, if we know anything about the end of time, we know that God will be faithful to his promises.

Whatever we make of the current environmental crisis, we cannot read it as a sign of the impending demise of creation. In the same way that God's hopes for creation were not destroyed by the fall, drowned by the flood or kidnapped by the Babylonians, neither are they fulfilled by climate change. From beginning to end the big story is ever hopeful, directed towards the renewal of creation. What's more, God's people are called to express his hope for creation in their

> But the day of the Lord will come like a thief. The heavens will disappear with a roar; the elements will be destroyed by fire, and the earth and everything in it will be laid bare.
>
> 2 Peter 3:10

> Behold, I will create new heavens and a new earth.
>
> Isaiah 65:17

> Then I saw a new heaven and a new earth, for the first heaven and the first earth had passed away…
>
> Revelation 21:1

Comment: As Jürgen Moltmann points out, Revelation says that God will make all things new, not that he will create all things from new.

> "I establish my covenant with you: Never again will all life be cut off by the waters of a flood; never again will there be a flood to destroy the earth." And God said, "This is the sign of the covenant I am making between me and you and every living creature with you, a covenant for all generations to come: I have set my rainbow in the clouds, and it will be the sign of the covenant between me and the earth."
>
> Genesis 9:11–13

Comment: Anxious that we should get the point, the phrase indicating that the covenant is between God and all living creatures of every kind on the earth is repeated five times in the space of one chapter.

THE BIG STORY

ONE
GOD
PEOPLE
HOPE 1
Celebrating the one true God

An inconvenient truth

Those with the power to change environmental policy have often resisted, due to their conviction that the economy will suffer as a result. Al Gore offers a different view. "Doing the right thing moves us forward," he says in *An Inconvenient Truth*, his documentary film about global warming.

The former vice president says that he considers global warming to be a moral issue and argues that doing the right thing will open up new possibilities for wealth and employment while doing nothing loses us the planet.

Summarising the key obstacles to action, Gore quotes Upton Sinclair: "It is difficult to get a man to understand something when his salary depends upon his not understanding it."

Gore says: "The struggle to save the global environment is in one way much more difficult than the struggle to vanquish Hitler, for this time the war is with ourselves. We are the enemy, just as we only have ourselves as allies."

At home

Creation is not ephemeral and unimportant – some way station until the eschaton – but rather our home, now and always.

Steven Bouma-Prediger, *For The Beauty Of The Earth*
(Baker Academic, 2001, page 77, second printing)

Will this earth be destroyed or renewed?

Puzzling question – we're used to a lot of the apocalyptic (hidden code) language in the sayings of Jesus and the Book of Revelation (such as Mark 13 and Revelation 20) which seem at face value to suggest that, at the end of time, nothing remains of the old earth and old heavens. But that's not how the whole Bible teaches us to think of it. We look for a new heaven and a new earth (Revelation 21), which is going be in continuity with what we have experienced in our corrupt yet desirable life on earth. All of the best that is in our earthly life will be there – and the key to understanding this is the theological theme of the kingdom of God.

Jesus came and proclaimed to the world that, in him, the kingdom of God had come (Mark 1:15). That kingdom is

nothing less than the rule and reign of God, inaugurated in Jesus – which will one day, in the person of Jesus be complete. That's the guarantee that the future is of a heaven and earth renewed, a full and recreated life in the presence and love of God, a creation that has been completely renewed, and people finding what it means to be utterly and truly human. Jesus himself will be present, and all that is evil will have been destroyed, while all that is good will have been transfigured. Beyond death, beyond the end of the world as we know it, is something else which will be both incomparably glorious and just a little strangely familiar.

Pete Broadbent
Bishop of Willesden,
Spring Harvest Leadership Team

own historical time and space. For Israel, this meant holding firm to faith in periods of turbulence and volatility. For us, it means expressing God's perfect plan for creation amidst great ecological disturbance and uncertainty.

2.3
Eschat-ecology

The government of the cosmos, as described in Isaiah 40, is not a dictatorship. God works out his purposes in heaven and earth through his creatures, so we cannot talk about God's hope and then carry on regardless. We are the agents of God's hope here and now, but what does this mean for the church with regard to the environment and ecology?

The global crisis presents God's people with both a critical challenge and a great opportunity. It is a chance for us to impact history and live up to our role as God's partners. The Bible says that God the Father created the world through his Son and by his Spirit. We pray to the Father, follow the Son and are filled with the Holy Spirit, so the church is home to the hope of creation.

The creative Spirit of God at work in us, transforming us into new creations, is not our private possession or the property of the church. The Spirit who hovered over the waters in the beginning of the big story will perfect creation at the end.

The Holy Spirit longs to equip the church to help in the healing and conservation of creation. The church is best qualified ideologically to meet the challenge because while others will become discouraged we know that God's creation is ordered and his history is hopeful. We look not to the future destruction of the planet but to its perfection, and so we should join with those groups that are working to save the planet.

Issues such as climate change, global warming, renewable energies, recycling, extinction of species, devastation of forests, etc. should be at the top of the church's agenda. Not because they are topical or trendy but because we are the creator's partners, the ones through whom the creator will perfect the world. We are the hope for the world's renewal. And remember, it's the only plan – there is no backup.

Many churches have entered God's 'ecomission' field. Green issues are talked about from the pulpit and in the pew, and Christians are creatively redesigning their lives to promote the planet. These visionaries in our midst are evidence

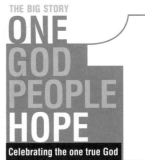

Hope Note:

Praying for creation

When we pray for the healing of the land, we apply the work of Christ on the cross to the creation.… . Just as in praying for an individual to come to faith, or in asking for healing, we pray … in the knowledge that the healing of the land is in line with God's will. We also pray in the knowledge that we may or may not see quick results, and that all healing comes by God's grace. Again, just as in praying for physical healing we encourage appropriate medical care alongside prayer, so in healing the land, prayer and practical action should go hand in hand. Prayer is not a substitute for good stewardship, and Christians who wish to see their local areas improved must be involved in practical conservation and environmental action as well as prayer.

Dave Bookless, *Theology of the Land*,
http://en.arocha.org/ukconsunday/index3.html

Hope in Verse:

The very thought

I love the very thought of Heaven:
Where angels sing
In perfect, perpetual Choir Practice.
Where Father, Son, and Spirit
Rule, unchallenged,
And are honoured in full measure.
I love the very thought of Heaven:
But I was not made
To live there

Gerard Kelly, *Spoken Worship*

image: www.freeimages.co.uk

Hope Note:

Living God's dream for creation

The implications of this are immense. In terms of ecological care, it challenges us to live our lives in such a way that we enable the rest of creation to fulfil its eschatological goal. This sounds very lofty and noble, but the reality is that we cannot espouse the eschatological theology that has been argued for in this chapter without it impacting our day-to-day living. So, for example, if I buy meat from animals that have been intensively farmed or if I buy vegetables that have needed the land to be drenched in chemicals to grow them, or flown thousands of miles across the world, then I am not living in a way that enables "creation's praise of the creator". On the other hand, if I buy my electricity from a 'green' supplier, take efforts to reduce the amount of packaging I use, press my local MP to support political reforms aimed at reducing CO_2 emissions and plant some trees on the green areas around my house then I am engaging in actions that will last into the future.

Ruth Valerio, "And there was no more sea", *What are we waiting for?*

10 Steps to save the world

1. Green your city

These ideas range from the very simple to the more complex – whatever level suits you. First, approach your local council with a clear offer: "We want to keep this city clean and attractive – we are offering to do the planning and the work. What can we do?"

- ADOPT A BLOCK: With a group, or two or three, decide to landscape a specific section of your city, perhaps the most run-down area. Some communities have 'adopt a block' programmes. If there isn't one, be the first to adopt a block in your area and be responsible for its upkeep.
- STAGE A CLEANUP: Offer a clean-up event with a group in an area of a city that needs it.
- PLANT A TREE: Plant trees on county-owned property that is unlikely to be developed. You will need to coordinate with city planners to find out the areas available and the types of trees/shrubs they would like to have planted.
- DO SOME LANDSCAPING, CREATE A PARK: Landscape a city monument or historical building. This allows for a lot of creative expression for budding gardeners. If space is available, perhaps landscape a park, a walk and sit kind of place – if land is designed well, you could include a small pond with ducks and fish.

2. Green your church/ workplace

- REDUCE PAPERWORK: Whenever possible, use PowerPoint slides instead of handouts.
- AVOID WASTE: Try to avoid waste at functions you coordinate. If possible, use re-useable plates, cups and cutlery.
- CREATE A RECYCLING SYSTEM: Find a system to collect all newspapers, magazines and used paper.

3. Noah's Ark

In theory, we'd all like to protect our animals and plants and maintain as great a diversity as possible. An estimate by The World Conservation Union suggests that we are destroying more than 16,000 species as a result of our lifestyles encroaching on their habitats. Get involved in all sorts of ways. Find out how at www.worldwildlife.org

4. Cut the rubbish

Part of the myth that drives over-consumption is that extra goods make our lives happier – the myth is too costly to the earth and to our souls.

- REFUSE OR REDUCE: Just say no to buying something you don't need – every time you buy something, you're using up a piece of the earth and causing pollution.
- REUSE OR RECYCLE: Try and create a second or third life for as much of your waste as possible.

5. Keep the air clean

Don't waste electricity. Electricity is mostly produced by burning coal, oil and gas and this action gives off carbon dioxide.

6. Take a bike/ walk/run

Car fumes produce carbon dioxide and nitrogen oxide – so try to cut down on car journeys if possible. Use a bike or walk – it's good exercise for you too!

7. Be kind to animals

People for the Ethical Treatment of Animals (PETA) campaigns against companies that violate animals. Learn which food and clothing products are created without animal testing and discover other resources for further education. (www.peta.org.uk)

8. Clean without chemicals

Some cleaning products containing chemicals and perfumes can actually be more harmful than the germs and dirt they are designed to get rid of, according to author Sheherazade Goldsmith in *A Slice of Organic Life* (Dorling Kindersley). Sheherazade suggests making your own cleaning products. For example, put vinegar in a squirt dispenser and use it to cut through grease and dirt on tiles and keep down mould growth, or try using coarse sea salt to clean the toilet bowl.

9. Buy locally

Cut down on food air miles by avoiding meat and vegetables that have been flown into the country from abroad. Instead, look for seasonal food that has been produced in the UK. Look out for farmers' markets, box schemes and farm shops in your area for true local produce.

10. Make your own food

Try to cut down on the amount of prepared food you buy. It's a healthier and a cheaper option, as well as being more eco-friendly by cutting down on transport and packaging costs. Cook up your own food in bulk and freeze for days when you are too busy to cook from scratch. You could also check out A Rocha's website for loads more ideas. (www.livinglightly24-1.org.uk)

Hopeful politics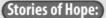

Engaging in issues of the environment is just one way of contributing to God's new creation. Andy Flannagan, the national songwriter/worship leader with Youth For Christ UK, has become involved in politics.

"From the age of nineteen I've known that God has called me to 'speak up for those who cannot speak for themselves'. After much procrastination, I joined a political party," Andy says.

"My local general committee met recently and myself and the other Christian represented one quarter of those present. Strategically important local decisions are made there! I've been able to hook church youth workers up with council representatives responsible for funding and help Christians to become involved in other local initiatives. Real relationships are brokered. My knowledge of the immediate needs and issues affecting my local community has increased exponentially. But it's hard work. I am forced to give a researched and reasoned defence of my views rather than simply shouting loudly.

"This is where hope hits the ground running. Working through the seemingly mundane details of local housing issues or parking is exactly what salt and light are all about. Salt crystals are small and they work themselves into the smallest fibres of the meat to preserve it. He is making all things new. Not just the stuff that grabs the headlines. When you spend time at an MP's surgery, you see face-to-face the unbelievable spectrum of needs in an area. Dealing with these issues is one of the hardest, most thankless and unglamourous jobs that I can imagine. To me that sounds a bit like carrying a cross."

of God's hope for creation. Caring for the environment will alleviate poverty, decrease infant mortality, reduce human trafficking, encourage enterprise, enable education and so forth. By serious engagement with environmental issues, we will bring closer God's hoped for renewing of the world. This doesn't mean God negates his responsibility by delegating all care for the creation. All things in time and space are held within God's sovereign care. However, as God's people we are called to imitate his care for the creation within our own time and space.

Our brothers and sisters in the Orthodox Church have a beautiful view of worship as the act of God's people giving the world back to its creator. As worshippers of the living God, we do not live in fear of what history may bring. Neither do we ignore creation as a temporary physical phenomenon. Through our work and worship, our lives and relationships, we hopefully hand every aspect of our world back to the Father.

Conclusion

Let's remind ourselves of the ground we have covered.

Hope for creation

- HERE ENDETH THE LESSON: The experience of exile causes Israel to question God's presence and faithfulness in the most honest way. God listens and responds to the challenges and allegations his people make with comfort and tenderness, not further judgment.

- IN THE BEGINNING, HOPE: By pointing her to creation, Isaiah reminds Israel that God had hopes for creation both before and after the fall. Because they hope in him, God's people should hope big.

- PAINTING THE PICTURE PERFECT: God's hopes for creation were not diminished by the fall. He intends to use humanity, the creatures who cursed creation, to perfect it. God's people can be encouraged that his hopes for them are not diminished by past failings.

Hope for new creation

- HOPE IN HISTORY: After the atrocities of the twentieth century, many have given up on hope. They have lost faith in our power to positively affect history and hope only for a quickening of God's direct and final intervention.

Certain Rumour by **Russell Rook**
Join Cleopas and the disciple with no name as they wander down the Emmaus Road with the risen Jesus. This book retells the big story of the Bible from the vantage point of the resurrection, and proves that it is a short walk to hope.

Questions of Hope:

People who die without belief in Jesus?

I will be honest. I really struggle with this question. I have many non-believing friends and Hindu family members who I would love to spend eternity with. I find views that say everybody will be saved very attractive.

However the Bible is clear: God differentiates between sheep and goats, wide and narrow paths, and the wise and foolish builders to name a few from Matthew's Gospel alone. The criteria for division will not be which church we go to, which Bible translation we use, or how many spiritual experiences we have had, but how we have responded to Jesus.

To those of us that are trusting in spiritual manifestations we have seen or experienced, Jesus says: "I never knew you. Away from me, you evildoers!" To those of us that just go with the flow Jesus says: "Small is the gate and narrow the road that leads to life, and only a few find it." To those of us that turn a blind eye to the needs of those around, Jesus

says: "They will go away to eternal punishment." To those of us who follow Mohammed, Dawkins, or Pastor X, Jesus says: "No-one comes to the Father except through me."

The Bible's teaching is difficult. But it is consistent with a God who loves us and is jealous for our love. It is consistent with a God who has gone to great lengths to rescue a rebellious world. It is consistent with a God who respects into eternity our free will choice to come in or stand away from his presence. It is consistent with a just God who knows our heart where nobody else does. It is consistent with a God of justice who cannot and will not turn a blind eye to evil.

I cannot change God's eternal and infallible word, however much I would like to. But this dichotomy motivates me to give my life to help people make their minds up about Jesus before they die.

Dr Krish Kandiah
Executive Director,
Churches in Mission

Hope Quote:

Giving the world back

The world was God's gift to us, existing not for its own sake but in order to be transformed, to become life, and so to be offered back as man's gift to God… Man was created as a priest: the world was created as the matter of a sacrament… If, therefore, we remember our nature and our origins, we shall see in that bread and wine placed upon the altar not merely our individual selves but the whole world… We place ourselves and the world upon the altar…and see there Christ: He stands at the centre and offers all to the Father.
Alexander Schmemann, *Church, World, Mission: Reflections on Orthodoxy and the West*
(St. Vladimir's Seminary Press, 1997) 224–225

Hope Quote:

Full salvation

The work of 'salvation', in its full sense, is (1) about whole human beings, not merely 'souls'; (2) about the present, not simply the future; and (3) about what God does through us, not merely what God does in and for us. If we can get this straight, we will rediscover the historic basis for the full-orbed mission of the church.
Tom Wright, *Surprised by Hope* (SPCK 2007)

One Hope DVD course
A six-session DVD resource that brings expert input, provocative panel discussions and inspiring stories into small groups. Covering the themes of the Spring Harvest week, One Hope is a great opportunity to consolidate learning and share Spring Harvest back home.

- THE ENDS OF THE EARTH: Ecological chaos is considered as evidence for the irreversible decline of human history and God's oncoming judgment in the destruction of the planet. However, at the end of the big story creation is renewed, not destroyed.

- ESCHAT-ECOLOGY: Filled with the Spirit and armed with the foresight of new creation, God's people are the most hopeful of all humanity. The environment represents one way in which the church can impact history by embracing and embodying God's hope for creation.

Final thoughts

The Bible provides a unique view of the scale and scope of human history, from its beginnings in a garden to its future completion with a new heaven and earth. When God created the world he said it was good, and he intended to perfect his creation with the help of humanity. God then watched as they threw his project into doubt. Rather than give up – on his project or his people – God still intends to use the now-fallen human race to fulfil his hopes for creation. The story of creation from beginning to end is an astonishingly hopeful story in which can be found the revelation of God and the key to all hopefulness.

The big story can restore hope to those who have lost faith in history. God's people can and do impact history, as the Christian tradition shows. As the people who have grasped God's plans for the future, our role in creation is vital. We are God's partners in bringing his tomorrow closer to our today, and our response to the ecological crisis is a perfect example of this. Having identified the problem in history and having understood that ecological ruin is not compatible with God's hopes for creation, we take it upon ourselves, by the power of the Spirit, to bring about change. In this we pray, "Your will be done, your kingdom come."

One final question, when can we expect the fulfilment of God's hope for creation? Paul writes that creation is groaning as it waits for the full and final coming of Christ's kingdom, using the image of a woman in labour painfully bringing new life into the world. Today's conclusion reinforces the lesson of yesterday. As with the coming of the kingdom and the last days, the new creation has already begun to take shape, starting with God's resurrection of Jesus. Through the resurrected Jesus and the power of his Spirit, God is making all things new. He is creating a new world around us and through us.

space for notes

THE BIG STORY

ONE
GOD
PEOPLE
HOPE

Celebrating the one true God

Recommended Reading

A Shorter Read

What Are We Waiting For?

Leading theologians and Christian thinkers discuss the issue of hope as it relates to theology, the Bible, the church and culture. The essays aim to provide a short and informative read.

"Eschat-Ecology" by Ruth Valerio

Helps us to understand God's good and perfect plan for creation and inspires us to put this theology into practice through ecologically clean living.

"Pop Culture" by Krish Kandiah

Dips into the world of film, music and fiction as it explores the eschatology that pervades contemporary culture and asks how we can bring God's word to life in a brave new world.

A Longer Read

Planetwise by Dave Bookless (Inter-Varsity Press)

Gives a powerful and accessible view of the theology of creation while providing a survey of the present ecological crisis and an environmental manifesto for the church.

A Lighter Read

L is for Lifestyle: Christian Living That Doesn't Cost the Earth
by Ruth Valerio (Inter-Varsity Press)

From bananas to investments, how to take better care of people and our planet, God's beloved creation.

A Deeper Read

Hope Against Hope: Christian Eschatology at the Turn of the Millennium
by Richard Bauckham and Trevor Hart (Eerdmans 1999)

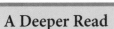

Two of the country's leading theologians bring together the themes of biblical theology, contemporary history and culture to stretch our understanding of God's hope.

A Book for all the Family

Change the World for a Fiver: We Are What We Do (Short Books 2004)

With stunning graphics and clever design, this quirky book provides fifty brilliant and easily applicable ideas for changing the world. The cover can be removed and used as a poster that illustrates the 50 ideas.
www.wearewhatwedo.org

Resources for churches

Carbon Fast Church Resource, available from Tearfund

Try out Tearfund's fun new Carbon Fast for Lent 2008 and save the world from climate change – or at least, show the government that we're willing to take action. Carbon Fast is the kind of thing your church or house group could do together. The resource includes 12 booklets and a poster. Go to www.tearfund.org.uk/carbonfast

ONE HOPE
OUT OF TOWN

space for notes

Hope out of town

Introduction

Having uncovered God's hopes for creation, we turn now to God's hopes for his people. History has often tested the hope of God's people. And, as Isaiah testifies, the periods of greatest testing were often the prelude to salvation. Today we will use three perspectives to look at how God's hope saved and sustained his people when they were far from home and out of town.

1. ISAIAH: The Jews who find hope in Isaiah 40–55 have a powerful story to tell about the power of God's hope when far from home.

2. THE EXODUS: By retelling the story of their ancestors, an exiled nation finds new hope.

3. THE CHURCH: As we remember our own salvation story, we encounter Christ and embody his hope for the future.

THE BIG STORY

ONE
GOD
PEOPLE
HOPE

Celebrating the one true God

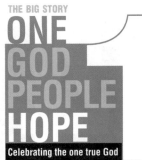

Teaching Block 1:

Back to Go

We begin with Israel out of town. In remembering their ancestors' miraculous escape from Egypt, the exiles long for another exodus. Three questions concern us...

- What does the story of the Exodus tell us about God's hopes for his people?
- Can we rely on the promises God has made?
- What does the future hold for those who hope in spite of their circumstances?

Teaching Block 2:

Becoming his Story

We will explore how God's story of hope unfolds in the lives of the disciples and the church. In particular we will look at...

- The new exodus led by Jesus during the first Easter weekend.
- The life of the church as an expression of God's hope for the whole world.
- The harsh and hopeful realities facing God's people in exile today.

Teaching Block 1:

Back to go

1.1
Remember, remember

> "Hear, you deaf; look, you blind, and see! Who is blind but my servant, and deaf like the messenger I send? Who is blind like the one committed to me, blind like the servant of the LORD? You have seen many things, but have paid no attention; your ears are open, but you hear nothing." It pleased the LORD for the sake of his righteousness to make his law great and glorious. But this is a people plundered and looted, all of them trapped in pits or hidden away in prisons. They have become plunder, with no-one to rescue them; they have been made loot, with no-one to say, "Send them back."
>
> Isaiah 42:18

Isaiah has provided us with a prophetic time machine. In Chapter 53 we returned to the events of the first Easter, and in Chapter 40 to the beginnings of creation. These journeys back in time may be a surprise, for prophecy and eschatology are largely considered futuristic affairs. Eschatology is, after all, the study of the 'last things' and prophecy is the attempt to predict the future. However, the Bible continually reminds us that the key to the future lies in the past and it isn't just the end of the big story that is eschatological or prophetic. The whole of history is driven by hope, therefore by ignoring what God has done yesterday we become blind and deaf to what he might do or say tomorrow. As God's people discover through history, we must often go back to the future.

In chapters 42–43, with Israel longing for a prophecy of liberation, Isaiah gives a history of the Exodus. But why? The Exodus is a definitive drama for God's people. To be an Israelite means that your ancestors tasted the unleavened bread of the Passover, fled across the parted sea, watched Pharaoh's armies perish in the waters, received God's commandments on Sinai, had their faith formed in the wilderness and inherited Jerusalem. At those times when an Israelite feels far from home or is experiencing an identity crisis, there is no better story than the Exodus.

> But now, this is what the LORD says – he who created you, O Jacob, he who formed you, O Israel: "Fear not, for I have redeemed you; I have summoned you by name; you are mine. When you pass through the waters, I will be with you; and when you pass through the rivers, they will not sweep over you. When you walk through the fire, you will not be burned; the flames will not set you ablaze. For I am the LORD, your God, the Holy One of Israel, your Saviour; I give Egypt for your ransom, Cush and Seba in your stead."
>
> Isaiah 43:1–3

In the same way that we say the Christian story began with Easter, the Jewish interpretation of history often places the start of their story with the Exodus. Only after coming to terms with this story can a Jew really understand creation, and so Israel has faithfully remembered and re-enacted the Passover since that miraculous night in Egypt. Re-staging the feast re-presents Israel's story and makes her ancestral hope of salvation real for a new generation.

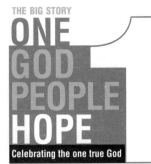
Will we meet again those who have died?

Of course! God's grace doesn't rub out our individual identity, but enhances and beautifies it. We don't know how we will meet after death, but the Bible promises that we will be "with Christ" (e.g. Phil 1:23), and if we are all with him, then it seems to follow that we'll be with each other, too! Then, when the new creation dawns, we will have new bodies to match (Paul calls it a "spiritual body", 1 Cor 15:44), like Jesus himself when he rose from death. Just as he was recognisable to his disciples, so will we be! Each of us, obviously and gloriously ourselves, united in enjoyment of God's new world. Revelation 21:1–22:5 is the biblical description of it.

It's possible to opt out, sadly. Rev 21:8 makes this clear. So we won't be together with any who turn out ultimately, before God, to be "the cowardly, the unbelieving, the vile,

the murderers, the sexually immoral, those who practise magic arts, the idolaters and all liars." If that's what we want to be, then finally God will respect our desire. Such is the dignity and value of our individual human identity – we can push the self-destruct button if we wish. But if we love our unbelieving friends and relatives, and pray for them, and carry them in our hearts, then at the last they could be like the paralysed man in Mark 2:1–12, carried into forgiveness before Jesus by the faith of his friends.

Look around you – you'll have to live with this lot for all eternity. Better start liking them.

Steve Motyer
Lecturer in New Testament & Hermeneutics,
London School of Theology

Spielberg's exodus

In a star-studded career, the prolific film-maker Stephen Spielberg has used an array of themes, settings and scenarios. And yet, time and again he returns to the Exodus. In *Schindler's List* we have a World War II re-enactment of the story as Oscar Schindler leads many Jews to safety from the jaws of Nazi concentration camps. In *Saving Private Ryan*, another World War II movie, we witness a kind of reverse take on the Exodus with a whole team of soldiers sent to liberate one member of their regiment. As if this were not enough, in 1998 Spielberg's film studio DreamWorks made *The Prince of Egypt*, an animated film that retells the story directly.

Remembering roots

There's a view… that in an age like ours, of unprecedented change, our values, too, must change… . It's a view that couldn't be more wrong. It's when the winds blow hardest that you need the deepest roots. When you're entering uncharted territory, it's when you need a compass to give you a sense of direction.
Chief Rabbi Jonathan Sacks, *From Optimism to Hope: Thoughts for the Day* (Continuum International 2004)

4 ONE HOPE
OUT OF TOWN

"Since you are precious and honoured in my sight, and because I love you, I will give men in exchange for you, and people in exchange for your life. Do not be afraid, for I am with you; I will bring your children from the east and gather you from the west. I will say to the north, 'Give them up!' and to the south, 'Do not hold them back.' Bring my sons from afar and my daughters from the ends of the earth – everyone who is called by my name, whom I created for my glory, whom I formed and made." Lead out those who have eyes but are blind, who have ears but are deaf. All the nations gather together and the peoples assemble. Which of them foretold this and proclaimed to us the former things? Let them bring in their witnesses to prove they were right, so that others may hear and say, "It is true." "You are my witnesses," declares the LORD, "and my servant whom I have chosen, so that you may know and believe me and understand that I am he. Before me no god was formed, nor will there be one after me. I, even I, am the LORD, and apart from me there is no saviour. I have revealed and saved and proclaimed – I, and not some foreign god among you. You are my witnesses," declares the LORD, "that I am God."

Isaiah: 43:4–12

Before the Exodus is Israel's story, it is first and foremost God's story. God reveals his character in the way in which he miraculously rescues, forgives, forms, sustains and provides for his people. By reading this story we discover what God is like. And by knowing who God is, as the creator and perfecter of all things, we find hope for the future.

For Isaiah, the Exodus provides fresh hope for the exiles. It assures them that Israel's future is not going to be decided in a cosmic lottery but is governed by the creator of history. National life is to be a journey towards the plans, purposes and place that God has for Israel. While there is often going to be hardship along the way, the destination is secure. The Exodus is a parable of God's hope that all people will find liberation and salvation, that all peoples will join the journey and become his people.

For those of us who, like Israel, sometimes grow impatient with the slow progress of our journey, the Exodus reveals an important truth. While the Israelites could have completed their trek in forty days, God took them the long way round. The forty years it took was the optimum time for God to transform a rabble into his people. Likewise Israel's extended period of exile in Babylon provided the opportunity to rediscover what it means to be God's chosen people. We should not be surprised if, as individuals and churches, it takes us time to realise God's hopes for us.

In the wilderness Israel discovered that God is not *timeless*. Although Christians sometimes talk about God's timelessness, this concept is alien to the big story. Timelessness, a construct of Greek philosophy, comprises a state outside of time and devoid of all temporality. A timeless god would be uninterested in history, stories or relationships. He literally would not have the time to rescue a nation, tell them his story or journey with them through a wilderness. What's more, a timeless god probably would not have time for creating in the first place.

In the wilderness Israel discovered that God, far from detaching himself from the hopes and fears of his people, had become intimately involved in their lives. God is more timely than timeless, which is why the Bible describes God as *eternal*. Eternal God transcends created time. Unlike us, he is not subject to the ticking clock, the rising and falling of the sun or the rhythmic pattern of the seasons. Yet he is the creator of time. Time is important to him. He doesn't work according to our schedules, but his own.

As with Israel so with us. God accompanies us on our journey and it is taking longer than we anticipated because of the frustrating hold-ups and unwanted detours. Our world treats time as just another commodity that we never have

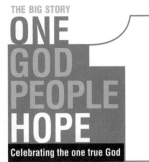

Hope in Verse:

The wanderer

Often the wanderer pleads for pity
And mercy from the Lord; but for a long time,
Sad in mind, he must dip his oars
Into icy waters, the lanes of the sea;
He must follow the paths of exile: fate is inflexible.

Anglo-Saxon poem, Anon.

Hope Quote:

Sabbath time

Keeping the Sabbath gives rise to a pattern of life not determined by the business cycle, the need for greater productivity, or the possibilities of technology (especially communications). Keeping the Sabbath reminds us that we are not in control of time, rather, time is part of God's good creation… Observing the Sabbath – itself an act of worship – interrupts our attempts to control our destinies, our anxieties about not having enough time, and our worries about how to spend our time usefully and calls us to participate in activities that appear useless to the world but are timely if creation is a gift whose time is fulfilled.

Luke Bretherton, "Mundane Holiness," eds. Andrew Walker & Luke Bretherton, *Remembering Our Future: Explorations in Deep Church* (Paternoster 2007)

Story of Hope:

The long minute

A man said to God, "How long is a minute to you?"

God replied, "To me a minute is as a thousand years and a thousand years is as a minute."

The man asked another question, "How much is a penny?"

God answered, "For me a penny is like a million pounds and a million pounds is just a penny."

The man paused, looking hopeful. "In that case, can I have a penny please?"

God smiled, looked at the man and replied, "Sure … just hang on a minute…"

Hope Note:

Exodus then Genesis

Jewish Rabbis and Christian theologians have long since suggested that it may be better to read Exodus before Genesis. God first and foremost, they say, wants a *people*. However, having decided to create such a community, he needs a place to put them and so creates the heavens and the earth.

Prayer in Hope:

Kiddush (Jewish Sabbath Prayer)

Blessed are You, Lord our God, King of the universe, who makes us holy through doing His commands, and delights in us. Willingly and with love He gives us His holy Sabbath to inherit, for it recalls the act of creation. This is the first day of holy gatherings, a reminder of the Exodus from Egypt. Because You chose us to be holy among all peoples, willingly and with love You gave us Your holy Sabbath to inherit. Blessed are You Lord, who makes the Sabbath holy.

enough of. We sometimes try to speed time up, expand it or make it go away, and in doing this we risk bypassing God. But God made everything for a purpose, including time. Creation takes time. Pastors frustrated at the slow growth of their flock, disciples discouraged with their retarded personal development, evangelists guilty at their lack of fruit, and churches disheartened by their small impact on their community should take heart. All these things take time, and though we never have enough of it God is eternal and has all the time in the world.

1.2
Promises, promises

In God, Israel's hopes for the future are secure. The Exodus theme continues as Isaiah 44 describes the promised land of the exiles, a land of plenty, rich and fruitful, whose fertility is sure to rub off on its inhabitants. Having whetted the people's appetite the prophet describes the happiest possible ending.

The importance of the *land* should not be overestimated even though Israel's faith and her capital are inextricably linked. Jerusalem is the centre of the Jewish universe, the meeting point of heaven and earth, but it is not simply the *land* that is important. It is also the *promise*.

Israel's journey with God is measured and mapped out by many promises. In fact, national life is the result of a promise. Many years before the Exodus, God assured an elderly Abram and his infertile wife, Sarah, that their progeny would one day outnumber the stars and bless every nation on earth. While he took his time about it, God came through on his promise and the exiles can identify the creator as the God who always keeps his promises. No matter how hard they find it to keep their side of the bargain, the people of Israel can guarantee that God will deliver on his promise.

The consequences of this are both reassuring and painful. Reassuring in that Israel's recognition of God's faithfulness forces her to live with the consequences of her actions. Having graciously warned us of the dangers of sin, God can no more remove the consequences of our sin than he can undo his warning. And painful in that it is this less-than-comfortable side of God's faithfulness that Israel must endure in exile.

Having been ignorant of the merciful warnings of the first thirty-nine chapters of Isaiah, Israel experiences the uncomfortable consequences of her sin. Isaiah

space for notes

But now listen, O Jacob, my servant, Israel, whom I have chosen. This is what the LORD says – he who made you, who formed you in the womb, and who will help you; Do not be afraid, O Jacob, my servant, Jeshurun, whom I have chosen. For I will pour out water on the thirsty land, and streams on the dry ground; I will pour out my Spirit on your offspring, and my blessing on your descendants. They will spring up like grass in a meadow, like poplar trees by flowing streams. One will say, 'I belong to the LORD'; another will call himself by the name of Jacob; still another will write on his hand, 'The LORD's', and will take the name Israel.

Isaiah: 44:1–5

By the rivers of Babylon we sat and wept when we remembered Zion.

Psalm 137:1

Comment: God's faithfulness, as Israel experiences in exile, cuts both ways. If God warns the nation that by rejecting her inheritance, calling and responsibilities she will forsake the attendant privileges, then his eternal faithfulness gives him no option but to allow his people to suffer the consequence of their own misguided actions.

Story of Hope:
Turn off your telly

A few decades ago many Salvationists would mark the Sabbath by, among other ways, draping a Salvation Army flag over their television set. The practice was eventually interpreted as outmoded asceticism (how dare one enjoy oneself on the Lord's day). However, what would happen if we were to turn off our televisions on Sunday and leave God to use the newly available time for something that he wants to do with us?

Song of Hope:

O God, our help in ages past,
our hope for years to come,
our shelter from the stormy blast,
and our eternal home:

O God, our help in ages past,
our hope for years to come,
be thou our guide while troubles last,
and our eternal home!

Isaac Watts (*Spring Harvest Praise 2007/08*)

Song of Hope:
Somewhere

If one song could sum up the life and work of Jewish composer Leonard Bernstein, it would be "Somewhere." In *West Side Story*, lyricist Stephen Sondheim perfectly describes the composer's aspiration when he writes: "There's a place for us, A time and place for us. Hold my hand and we're halfway there. Hold my hand and I'll take you there, Somehow, Someday, Somewhere!"

Hope Note:
Keeping a promise

The concept of promise is essential to relationships the world over. If I promise my wife that I will take out the rubbish, then she expects me to do it. If I do not live up to my promise, this failure will impact our relationship. If I go further and break more significant and substantial promises – promises of fidelity, parental responsibility, the provision of income, support and friendship – then at some point our relationship will hit the rocks. Our marriage is only as good as the promises we made.

Hope Quote:
Beauty in darkness

There is beauty in the dark valleys of life. It is called hope.

Joan D. Chittister, *Scarred by Struggle, Transformed by Hope* (Eerdmans 2005)

Comment: "Israel understood the dynamics of empire and imagination and always had a counter plan. In the shadow of the empire, Israel's prophets wrote evocative and subversive poetry that wove together images of homecoming and restoration … and a coming Messiah who would do a new thing."

Brian J. Walsh & Sylvia C. Keesmaat, *Colossians Remixed: Subverting the Empire* (Authentic Media, 2005,) 82

now reassures Israel, by remembering the promises made to her ancestors, that God's faithfulness is unconditional. What's more, by retelling the story of the Exodus he raises the expectation of liberation. As with her ancestors in the wilderness, the period between promise and fulfilment, between exile and homecoming is an opportunity for spiritual formation and faithfulness. In this, Israel anticipates our experience of the tension between the now and not yet of God's kingdom.

In an instantaneous society, the lessons of the Exodus and exile are precious. Those who measure success by early arrival or immediate answer to prayer find themselves continually frustrated and disappointed. In spiritual terms, the pursuit of instant gratification is exhausting and unsustainable. To be God's chosen people means learning to live with him on the road and remembering that reaching the promised destination entails a commitment to travel.

Many of those who experienced the Exodus or were exiles in Babylon never saw the promised land, yet this didn't invalidate their faith, cancel their contributions or diminish their testimony. Far from being hopeless, their willingness to lay down their lives for the hope of future generations made them the most hopeful people in history. In a time when it was easy to forget, they kept telling the old stories as promises of what was to come.

"I am the LORD, your Holy One, Israel's Creator, your King." This is what the LORD says – he who made a way through the sea, a path through the mighty waters, who drew out the chariots and horses, the army and reinforcements together, and they lay there, never to rise again, extinguished, snuffed out like a wick: "Forget the former things; do not dwell on the past. See, I am doing a new thing! Now it springs up; do you not perceive it? I am making a way in the desert and streams in the wasteland."

Isaiah 43:15–19

1.3
Tomorrow, tomorrow

It's time for a twist. Having reminded Israel of the Exodus, Isaiah now tells her to forget all about it. The prophet is anxious not to miss God's future by becoming stuck in the past. Isaiah's rendition of the Exodus is not a reminder of the old days but a prophecy for the future. What's more, this new walk to freedom will look very different and Isaiah wants Israel to recognise it. Throughout the history of God's people, we have found it too easy to become stuck in the past and miss the new thing God wants to do.

The Passover, which commemorates Israel's escape from Egypt, is a forward-thinking celebration. God instructed Moses to celebrate the first Passover prior to liberation. They party in hope, and then God delivers the people from Pharaoh. This festival of Israel's freedom is an opportunity for God's people to stand up and be counted. By invoking the Exodus, Isaiah is attempting to get the celebrations started in Babylon. In the same way that Israel's first Passover

Comment: Isaiah 47 and 48 continually juxtapose Babylon and Egypt against Israel. In Chapter 48, God goes so far as to instruct the Israelites to go out and leave Babylon behind.

North and Luton M 1

Questions of Hope:

What happens when we die?

The ultimate Christian hope is the resurrection of the body at the return of the Lord Jesus (see 1 Cor 15, for example). Bishop NT Wright calls this "life after life-after-death".

So what happens to people's souls when they die before the Lord returns, the in-between stage, also called "the intermediate state"? In the history of the church, a minority report has suggested some form of soul sleep, based on the sleep metaphor of death (see, for instance, 1 Thes 4:14,15).

Others have suggested that at personal death people are no longer in time but are somehow fast forwarded to the Last Day and so are 'resurrected at death'.

The majority report, however, asserts that death temporarily sunders our body/soul unity. At death, "the dust returns to the ground it came from, and the spirit returns to God who gave it" (Eccl 12:7). For the believer, this is what is meant by going to heaven when we die.

It is what Paul had in mind when he said that death was a departing to "be with Christ, which is better by far" (Phil 1:23 and see 2 Cor 5:8). Likewise, Jesus promised the penitent thief, "today you will be with me in paradise" (Lk 23:43).

The dark side of hope is that not only the righteous will be raised but also the unrighteous (see Acts 24:15). In their interval, they are held "for the day of judgment" (2 Pet 2:9).

Steve Brady
Principal,
Moorlands College

ROBIN WILLIAMS
PATCH ADAMS
BASED ON A TRUE STORY

Scenes of Hope:

Coming home

In the closing moments of the film *Patch Adams*, the medical student played by actor Robin Williams declares: "All of life is a coming home. Salesmen, secretaries, coal miners, beekeepers, sword swallowers, all of us. All the restless hearts of the world, all trying to find a way home. … Home. The dictionary defines it as both a place of origin and a goal or destination."

Hope Quote:

Tomorrow today

Hope is rooted in the past but believes in the future. God's world is in God's hands, hope says, and therefore cannot possibly be hopeless. Life, already fulfilled in God, is only the process of coming to realize that we have been given everything we need to come to fullness of life, both here and hereafter. The greater the hope, the greater the appreciation of life now, the greater the confidence in the future, whatever it is.

Joan Chittister, *Scarred by Struggle, Transformed by Hope*

Using the diagram opposite, complete your own 'life tree'.

This is an exercise in memory and testimony. Use the branches, trunk, leaves, etc. to review and display the formative experiences, encounters, people and places that have contributed to making you who you are today. Take time to thank God for his presence in your journey so far, whether noticed or not, and for the way he has used these aspects of your history to reveal his plans and purposes to you.

anticipated liberation, re-enactment of the Passover anticipates the salvation of God's people.

The Exodus story is a lesson for Israel to keep alert for God's future action. For this reason, Isaiah gives the exiles the title role and tells the story in the future tense. "When you pass through the waters, I will be with you." The Israelites can now look forward to their own liberation and their return to the promised land.

As we reflect upon God's active involvement in our past, we too should be encouraged. Christian testimony is more than reminiscing. Our stories comprise praise for the past and signs to the future. By remembering what God did yesterday and acknowledging his faithfulness today we become expectant about tomorrow. Because every promise that God makes is eternal, it is kept and fulfilled many times over. Every miracle is a signpost to God's future for us.

It is obviously no coincidence that the events of the first Easter coincided with Passover. This great celebration in anticipation was to be fulfilled through Jesus. Jews in the first century, certain New Testament scholars say, believed they were in exile.

At the Last Supper, Jesus celebrated the Passover with his disciples. All previous Passover festivals, whether celebrated in Egypt, the wilderness, the promised land or exile, were advance celebrations of this one event. As in Isaiah, the story is told in the future tense. Jesus casts himself as Moses in the leading role as he will lead creation to liberation. However, with every available animal being readied for the feast Jesus also plays the role of the sacrificial lamb. He is the Lamb of God who takes away the sins of the world.

In this moment God made a new and unconditional promise to save his people once and for all. He transformed the final meal of a condemned man, Jesus, his suffering servant, into an eternal banquet and his execution into a coronation. Because of this day we can be sure that there is nothing God would not do, or has not done, to bring hope. This meal is the fulfilment of God's faithfulness and the beginning of his kingdom on earth.

space for notes

"When you pass through the waters, I will be with you; and when you pass through the rivers, they will not sweep over you. When you walk through the fire, you will not be burned; the flames will not set you ablaze. For I am the LORD, your God, the Holy One of Israel, your Saviour; I give Egypt for your ransom, Cush and Seba in your stead."

Isaiah 43:2–3

Comment: "He says, I will make a way in the wilderness (Isa 43:19). We say that this *way* is either the divine and saving preaching for the gospel or perhaps Christ himself. For we have heard him say plainly, *I am the Way* (John 14:6)."
Cyril of Alexandria, cited in Robert Louis Wilken (ed. trans.), *Isaiah: Interpreted by Early Christian and Medieval Commentators* (Eerdmans, 2007) 310

Comment: As Tom Wright points out, Jesus fulfils Israel's Exodus hope in his resurrection. "Within the first-century world of Jesus, the Pharisees and the Sadducees, the doctrine of resurrection was a *revolutionary* doctrine. It spoke of God's determination to bring about the new Exodus, the real return from Exile, the great liberation from oppression and slavery, the liberation for which Israel longed."
Tom Wright, *Surprised by Hope* (SPCK, 2007)

"The wild animals honour me, the jackals and the owls, because I provide water in the desert and streams in the wasteland, to give drink to my people, my chosen, the people I formed for myself that they may proclaim my praise."

Isaiah 43:20–21

Agnus Dei

The church celebrates Christ's fulfilment of the Passover feast in one of her most famous prayers, the *Agnus Dei*, based on John 1:29.

Lamb of God,
you take away the sin of the world,
have mercy on us.

Lamb of God,
you take away the sin of the world,
have mercy on us.

Lamb of God,
you take away the sin of the world,
grant us peace.

Common Worship, Order One, Eucharistic Prayer G

Easter

Via the Jewish Passover, the Christian Easter has its roots far back in the history of religions, in the realm of the so-called natural religions. I am always struck by the emphasis Jesus places during his earthly journey on his "hour". He is going toward his death, but he avoids it until this hour has come. In this way he quite deliberately links his mission with mankind's whole history of belief and with the signs to be found in creation. He ties the accomplishment of his mission to this particular feast and, hence, to the first full moon of spring. To those who look at things only from the point of view of technology or historicism, this must appear unintelligible and devoid of meaning. But Jesus thought otherwise. By linking his hour to the revolutions of the moon and the earth, to the cycles of nature, he situates his death in a cosmic context and, conversely, relates the cosmos to man. We can understand ourselves, and Christ, properly only if we also learn how to listen to the voice of creation.

Pope Benedict XVI, *Images of Hope* (Ignatius Press 2006)

Teaching Block 2:

Becoming his story

2.1
Moving in with God

> While they were eating, Jesus took bread, gave thanks and broke it, and gave it to his disciples, saying, "Take and eat; this is my body." Then he took the cup, gave thanks and offered it to them, saying, "Drink from it, all of you. This is my blood of the covenant, which is poured out for many for the forgiveness of sins."
> Matthew 26:26–28

When it celebrates the Lord's Supper, or communion, the church re-enacts the Passover meal that Jesus shared with his disciples. This is also a celebration of our own exodus from darkness to light, from captivity to liberation, when we remember what Jesus has done and anticipate his coming. It is both an historical reconstruction of the Last Supper and a prophetic foretaste of the heavenly banquet.

One of us plays Jesus, breaking bread and pouring wine. The rest play disciples, hoping and praying that we can live faithfully. This is not amateur dramatics. As we revisit the events of the last supper, Christ visits us by the power of his Spirit. As we anticipate Christ's return, the Holy Spirit makes the risen Jesus present. By eating and drinking, we are accepting Christ's invitation to follow him to the end of the world and writing ourselves into the plot of the big story.

Through the first Passover in Egypt, Israel confirmed her part in God's story. By remembering this story in Babylon, the exiles hoped they might still have a part to play. As we re-enact the Last Supper we proclaim the climax of the big story and look forward to its hopeful and happy ending. As his people, we invest our lives in faithfulness with confidence in God's eternal capacity to keep promises. Our past, present and future lie in his plan for creation. Every moment is an opportunity to tell his story, embody his love and manifest his kingdom.

The role of the church is not simply to celebrate communion but to invite the world to celebrate communion. Since many people find church ritual obscure and alienating, we must find new ways of re-enacting God's story, of ensuring that our communities are included in the celebration of Christ's life, death and resurrection.

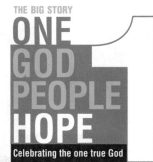

THE BIG STORY
ONE
GOD
PEOPLE
HOPE
Celebrating the one true God
1

Hope in Verse:

Breadsong

It's not in the bread
but in the breaking
that the mystery of God's story is told.
It's not in the seed
but in the dying,
not in the treasure
but in the digging for it.
It's not in the mountain
but in its moving.

It's not in the wine
but in the pouring out
that a new world is purchased
for the weary.
It's not in the cross
but in the crucified,
not in the nails
but in the nailing.
It's not in the grave
but in the rising from it.

It's in the giving
that the gift becomes life;
it's in the living
that the Word becomes flesh.

It's in this taking,
this receiving,
this sharing of a supper,
this pointing to a future
that is promised
and paid for
and pressed into our hands;
it's in this everyday mealtime miracle
that the universe is born
to new life.

Gerard Kelly, *Spoken Worship*

Stories of Hope:

Holy Communion in Iraq

The Christians in Baghdad gave me so much hope for the church. … Hundreds of Christians from all over the Middle East had gotten together – Catholic, Protestant, Orthodox. They read a statement from the Christian church directed to the Muslim community, declaring that they love them and believe they were created in the image of God. Then we sang familiar songs like "Amazing Grace." We said the Lord's Prayer in several languages. They led us to the cross and prayed a prayer similar to the one Jesus prayed when he was on the cross: "Forgive us, for we know not what we are doing." Hundreds and hundreds of people continued to try to get into the service and ended up gathering outside with candles. It was holy.

Shane Claiborne, *The Irresistible Revolution* (Zondervan 2006)

Hope Quote:

Hungry for Communion

Jesus becomes the food of life for his followers when they come into a new life and discover that it is by living for others that they find fulfilment of their own being.

Monika Hellwig, *The Eucharist and the Hunger of the World* (Sheed & Ward 2000)

Isaiah sees the new exodus as more than a return from exile in Babylon. He sees it as a way for every nation on earth to join the party in the new Jerusalem, and hopes all the peoples of the world will realise they have a part to play in the big story. Israel is the central player, she is called to be a blessing to all and a light for the Gentiles. Her failure on this front led, in part, to her exile. Armed with the poetry and songs of Isaiah she began to fulfil this role in a startlingly new way. How might our churches find new ways of calling others to join the drama of God's story?

Remembering what Christ has done reminds us how far we have to go. Our pale imitations of the gospel, frequent sins and petty idolatries cause us to question our part in God's story. Throughout the big story, God's people live as both settlers and nomads. The tension between these lifestyles is crucial. God's intervention in Egypt led the Hebrew people into a period of nomadic wandering, suggesting that salvation is about departure as much as arrival. It was by design that some of Israel's greatest moments came far from home. It is often when they think they have arrived that God's people are in the greatest danger, as the years preceding the exile show.

To every generation, Christian discipleship presents a fresh challenge. Following Jesus is inevitably different in each time and place – the saviour is the same, but the implications for our everyday lives vary significantly. A Christian who is happy to rest in the knowledge that their salvation is assured in Christ is the equivalent of a Hebrew slave celebrating the Passover in Egypt but never crossing the sea and journeying towards the promised land. We must keep on the move, invest in spiritual formation, deepen our biblical understanding and become better equipped to live out God's story in our world. God is making us into his people and leading us to the promised land, his kingdom.

By placing our hope in Jesus, we can be sure of our eternal destiny. Our future is found in the one who rose from the dead and rules the world, and yet we also know that we have a long way to go. In Christ, the final destination of creation is the start of an eternal journey.

2.2
Eternally open ended

In the same way that the Easter story provides a vision of our future, Isaiah's retelling of the Exodus brings the exiles hope of a happy ending. One day, according to the prophet, they will hold a party in the new Jerusalem. The book

"I am the living bread that came down from heaven. If anyone eats of this bread, he will live for ever. This bread is my flesh, which I will give for the life of the world."

John 6:51

THE BIG STORY

ONE
GOD
PEOPLE
HOPE

Celebrating the one true God

Hope Note:

Sharing Christ's cup

Henri Nouwen's *Can You Drink the Cup* is a reflection on Jesus' question to Zebedee's sons: "You don't know what you are asking, Jesus said to them. Can you drink the cup I am going to drink?" (Matt 20:22)

If we drink, we choose to share in the life of Christ, in all the joys, all the sufferings, all the responsibilities, all the truths, and all the hope that drinking the cup implies. Nouwen says that drinking the blood of Christ is "the full celebration of being human."

Hope Quote:

Walking into God

Donald Miller points out in *Blue Like Jazz* that as we journey towards God's future, he walks towards us.

"I am early in my story, but I believe I will stretch out into eternity and in heaven I will reflect upon these early days, these days when it seemed God was down a dirt road, walking towards me," he says. "Years ago He was a singing speck in the distance; now He is close enough I can hear his singing. Soon I will see the lines on His face."

Prayer for Hope:

Eternity now

I determine amidst all uncertainty always to trust
I choose to live beyond regret, and let you recreate my life
I believe You will make a way for me
And provide for me
If only I trust
And obey.
I will trust in the darkness and know that my times are still in Your hand.
I will believe You for my future,
chapter by chapter, until all the story is written.
…….. Teach me to live with eternity in view,
Tune my spirit to the music of heaven.

St. Brendan

4 ONE HOPE
OUT OF TOWN

space for notes

"Before me no god was formed, nor will there be one after me."

Isaiah 43:10[b]

Comment: "'Do not remember the former things … I am about to do a new thing' is thus a poignant call to wake up to the contemporaneity of faith. It is a challenge to muster sufficient theological imagination to see how divine purpose is unfolding."

Paul D. Hanson, *Isaiah 40–66*
(Interpretation Bible Commentaries)
(Westminster/John Knox Press, 1995), 74

of Revelation re-paints this as an eternal banquet at the end of time. In this way, the Passover and the Lord's Supper are a foretaste of communion with God, celebrations of a futuristic faith.

We often think and talk of God in the past tense. When we mean the one who pre-exists creation, this is justifiable. But God as the creator of the ends of the earth can also be referred to in the future tense. As the creator, God has journeyed with creation from the start. As the one who holds the ends of the earth, God comes to us from the future. The future belongs to God, leading theologians to talk about God living in the future. Our travels through time and history are taking us towards him.

God's people have often found it easier to live in the past than in the present or future. We too easily exchange a miraculous future for yesterday's comforts. With our worldview no longer dominant, we often hunger after the good old days and before long we become stuck in the past. Our traditions grow tired and our story is ignored. However, God holds the future so he is not threatened by this. He longs for us to find bold and daring ways to retell his story.

It is time for the church, like Isaiah, to sing a new song in a strange and foreign land. The music may not be familiar, or even comfortable on the ear, but we need to demonstrate our faithfulness to the God of the future. Jesus guarantees the church's continuation, but not its model. The New Testament clearly shows a number of very different types and styles of church, each focused on bringing the life and presence of Christ into a specific community. The big story teaches us that the twenty-first century church will, and should, look different. Our faith must resist easy comforts and get fit for the purposes of our futuristic God.

God has a futuristic perspective. He sees our past, present and future. He knows what he has done and what he plans to do, and he identifies us by our future. God doesn't see me as the person who messed up yesterday but as the one in whom he works today and who will be more like him tomorrow. He sees all the possibilities and opportunities that Jesus opened up for us. He doesn't see us as we were but as we will be when his Spirit's work in us is complete. Likewise, God's vision for the church is not a repeat of yesterday but a brand new tomorrow.

Our identity is not fixed by the mistakes of the past, our start needn't be our story. When we enter into a relationship with the King of creation we open every aspect of our lives to his perfect plans and purposes, and all things become possible. Following the events of Easter, the new day of creation began.

Hope Quote:

Faith on the move

The nomad does not live within the cycle of seed-time and harvest, but in the world of migration. This inspiring, guiding, protecting God of the nomads differs quite fundamentally in various respects from the gods of the agrarian peoples. The gods of the nations are locally bound. The … God of the nomads, however, is not bound territorially and locally. He journeys along with them, is himself on the move. The result of this is a different understanding of existence: Here existence is felt as history. This God leads men to a future which is not mere repetition and confirmation of the present, but is the goal of the events that are now taking place.

Jürgen Moltmann, *Theology of Hope*

Scenes of Hope:

Harmony in heaven

Swedish director Kay Pollak's film *Så som i himmelen* (*As It Is in Heaven*, 2004) tells the story of Daniel Daréus (Michael Nyqvist), a successful international conductor who returns to the small village in northern Sweden where he grew up to recuperate after a heart attack. The musical celebrity is soon recruited to conduct the church choir. In their attempt to produce a harmonious sound the singers have first to resolve the dissonances in their lives. Broken relationships must be reconciled, injustices put right and the excluded included before the choir can achieve true harmony. Ironically, as the power of music transforms them, the choir members find themselves ostracised from the church. For the minister and his elders, the choir's celebrations are too joyous, their music too adventurous and their lives too transformed for the well-established patterns of church life.

In the final scene, choirs from all over the world gather for an international competition. Now without their famed maestro, the choir must make music on their own. A member of the choir who suffers from severe learning difficulties begins to groan. Other members of the choir pick a note of their own and sing around him. Within the next moments the choir and every member of the audience join in creating the loudest and most powerful chord possible. Following the ascension of Christ, the church, no matter how broken, is called to lead the world in worship, to help all creation find its note of prayer and praise.

Sketchpad

Dickens' ghosts

Imagine yourself as Ebeneezer Scrooge, the main character in Charles Dickens' 1843 novel *A Christmas Carol*.

If the Ghost of Christmas Future were to visit you today, what vision of your future would you like him to outline? What do you want to achieve over the next twenty years? Where will your calling and vocation take you? Having jotted down, scribbled or sketched your preferred vision of the future, what must you do in the present to make these things possible?

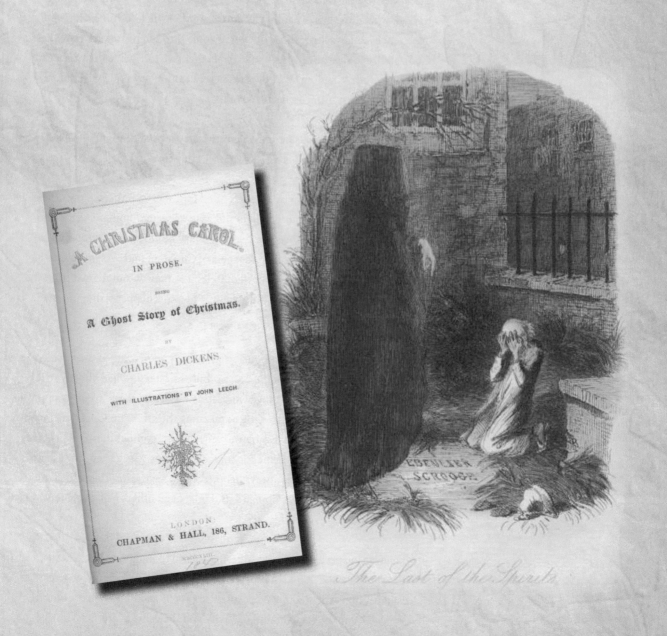

The Last of the Spirits

ONE HOPE
OUT OF TOWN

We are divine works in progress, with God making us into his image in the time he has made for us. Ultimately, our destiny is wrapped up in God's plan.

2.3
Exiles now

The story of God's people is always hopeful, whether in Egypt or Babylon, in the wilderness or Jerusalem, in the early church or today. The future belongs to God, who alone has the authority and power by which to rule history. Our experiences today mirror those of God's people through history as we witness God's ability to save and perfect. Like Israel then, we today live in the now and not yet of God's kingdom. We have the eternal assurance of our salvation now but recognise that miracles lie ahead of us.

The importance of hope is hard to overestimate. Hope at times of great suffering is the key to keeping on. It is a belief that we cling to.

Today, more Christians are being persecuted for their faith than at any other time in history. Many of our brothers and sisters live in a similar situation to that of the exiles, where Christianity is not illegal but local legislation makes it difficult, or impossible, to express tenets of Christian faith. As in Isaiah, believers are tolerated, even supported, so long as they do not detract from the dominant religious or political worldview. When this happens, they are made to suffer.

> Now when Daniel learned that the decree had been published, he went home to his upstairs room where the windows opened toward Jerusalem. Three times a day he got down on his knees and prayed, giving thanks to his God, just as he had done before. Then these men went as a group and found Daniel praying and asking God for help. … So the king gave the order, and they brought Daniel and threw him into the lions' den. The king said to Daniel, "May your God, whom you serve continually, rescue you!"
>
> Daniel 6:10,11,16

For the exiles in Babylon, this occurred when they were ordered to worship a local deity cast in the shape of the king. While the Israelites had already made many compromises in this strange world, this was a step too far. Worshipping an idol would be a denial of their identity, meaning they were no longer one people chosen by the one true God. Numerous current-day regimes permit Christians as long as they do not blaspheme the indigenous gods. Since we believe there is only one God, a Christian is always liable to break such laws. The bold claims of our faith about the one true God and its denial of all others will create tensions in many cultures.

If you haven't experienced it, the suffering is hard to imagine and the testimonies are often shocking. The cost of faith in a hostile environment gives Christians unprecedented hope because it shows us examples of hope among the hopeless, courage, freedom in captivity and the value of eternal security over temporary comfort. God's people staked their lives on the God who owns

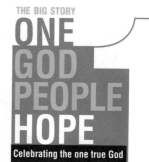

Story of Hope:

Transforming darkness

Darkest England & The Way Back In by Gary Bishop includes the account of a woman called Kim. She was a heroin addict, and over a number of years he and his wife helped and supported her through her habit. Kim gave birth to a daughter, Ann, but when it became obvious that Kim was returning to heroin, Gary and his wife felt compelled to inform Social Services for the sake of Ann's safety. The social worker divulged their identity to Kim, and as a result of this they suffered a series of verbal threats and acts of vandalism. Their relationship was never the same again, as the book explains:

"A few weeks after things had died down I saw Kim with Ann just down the street from the church, and as I approached I was longing for her to look up and speak to me… my heart was racing with hopeful anticipation as I got closer, then she looked up, saw me coming and quickly looked away. She turned her back on me, refusing to give me eye contact, and ushered Ann away down a side street. I felt like a bit of my heart scurried off after them.

"And as I wept during the rest of my walk down the street, something dawned on me. I came to Openshaw full of dreams and ideas about transforming the community … However, what I began to realise … was that in many cases the transformation that has taken place has been far more inside me than inside the different characters that I have come into contact with: Kim went back to her life as if she had never met us, but we will never go back to the way our life was before we met her."

Gary Bishop, *In Darkest England and the way back in*, 89–93

Hope Quote:

Evil

If all evil were prevented, much good would be absent from the universe. A lion would cease to live, if there were no slaying of animals; and there would be no patient martyrs if there were no tyrannical persecution.

Thomas Aquinas, *Summa Theologicae*, 1.22.2

Hope Note:

Facing facts

Many Christians around the world find themselves exiled at home and abroad.

- PERSECUTION OF CHRISTIANS is the largest human rights issue in today's world.
- OVER 200 MILLION CHRISTIANS in at least 60 countries are denied fundamental human rights solely because of their faith, according to World Evangelical Alliance.
- ONE CHRISTIAN IN TEN lives with persecution.

Picture of Hope:

Exiled hope

In the map right, areas marked in red denote the parts of the world where the practice of faith in Christ marks believers out for persecution.

http://www.opendoorsuk.org/

the future in the Exodus and the exile, and now our persecuted brothers and sisters are doing the same. According to Revelation, this costly faith is used by God to fulfil his hopes for the world in the final battle, which is won by an all-conquering army of martyrs.

Isaiah proves that the story of God's people will provide endless hope for the world. Their miraculous and steadfast faith around the world and throughout history changes our perspective on hope. How might God's people become part of our story? How can we be part of God's plan to fulfil his hope for them?

It is time for those of us who worship in comfort to tell the story of our persecuted brothers and sisters. By calling others to prayer and protest, to aid and advocacy we may assure them that their hope is not in vain.

> They overcame him by the blood of the Lamb and by the word of their testimony; they did not love their lives so much as to shrink from death.
>
> Revelation 12:11

space for notes

Conclusion

Let's remind ourselves of the story we've been telling…

Back to go

- REMEMBER, REMEMBER: Isaiah reminds Israel of the Exodus, God's work in her history. By retelling this story, God's people are reassured of God's intimate involvement in their lives and community.

- PROMISES, PROMISES: By re-enacting the stories of the past, Israel is reminded of God's continual faithfulness. God's people exist because God makes and keeps his promises.

- TOMORROW, TOMORROW: Having reminded them, Isaiah asks Israel to forget the former things. The miracles of history are not the end of the story. God can do even greater things tomorrow than he did yesterday.

Becoming his story

- MOVING IN WITH GOD: Christians celebrate Easter as the story of our own exodus. In Jesus, God's story of salvation and transformation becomes our story. By living out the good news of the gospel we become his story for the world.

- ETERNALLY OPEN ENDED: No matter how certain or secure we are in our faith, as God's people we are forever on the move. Our story is defined not by our start but by the plans that God has for us. We are divine works in progress.

Certain Rumour **by Russell Rook**
Join Cleopas and the disciple with no name as they wander down the Emmaus Road with the risen Jesus. This book retells the big story of the Bible from the vantage point of the resurrection, and proves that it is a short walk to hope.

THE BIG STORY
ONE
GOD
PEOPLE
HOPE
1
Celebrating the one true God
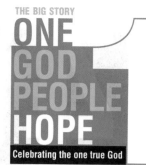

Stories of Hope:

Sentenced to death

The Christian community is not very large in Pakistan, and we face a lot of hostility from the Muslim population, particularly if we have converted from Islam. Some time ago I was sentenced to death under Pakistan's blasphemy laws and have been in prison ever since. At the time I was mourning the death of my nephew. One night my Muslim neighbours were singing very loudly, so I asked them if they could keep the noise down. They were very aggressive in their response and beat me, accusing me of blaspheming against the Prophet Mohammed. They then filed the claim which sent me to prison. In Pakistan, when a Muslim accuses someone of blasphemy, there is no need for any evidence to support the accusation.

The other prisoners threaten and beat me... Already [Muslim extremists] threaten my family on a daily basis... If they execute me, I will be the first person in Pakistan to have a death sentence for blasphemy carried through. But some who have been acquitted have already been murdered in backlashes from extremists, so even if I'm freed, I will have to spend the rest of my life in hiding.

In many ways I am very lucky. I have a group of Christian lawyers working on my case, even though it puts them and their families at risk. I am so grateful for the sacrifices they have made to ensure that innocent people are protected. I love my country, but it is not safe for Christians here. Every day we live our lives looking over one shoulder, often keeping our faith secret for fear that we may be attacked...

I have hope that justice will prevail, but victory is not always close at hand. Please pray for me and my country.

Yours in Christ,
Younis Masih

Postcard to a Spring Harvest guest, reprinted with permission

Exercising Hope:

Can I tell you a story?

The words above make for an unusual postcard. Younis Masih is someone for whom God's hope is the most precious and vital resource. Life and faith would be impossible without it.

Try this exercise; share a postcard from a persecuted Christian with three friends, colleagues, neighbours or family members.

By remembering their story and retelling it you can not only share God's hope with others but also invite them to become carriers of this same hope. By sharing the story, we not only anticipate the freedom which is the future of God's people but invite others to work towards that freedom in the here and now. Having shared the story, ask these three friends to join you in prayer, advocacy, protest, etc.

For more information contact Christian Solidarity Worldwide (www.csw.org.uk)

One Hope DVD course
A six-session DVD resource that brings expert input, provocative panel discussions and inspiring stories into small groups. Covering the themes of the Spring Harvest week, One Hope is a great opportunity to consolidate learning and share Spring Harvest back home.

space for notes

● EXILES NOW: God's hope for the future often shines brightest in those that others would consider hopeless. The unquenchable hope of the persecuted church challenges us to become the answer to their prayers.

Final thoughts

Having reminded Israel of her story, God calls Israel to testify to the heavens and the earth that he is the one God, the maker of heaven and earth. What a turnaround for this besieged and beaten bunch, who become the means by which God demonstrates his power once and for all. Just in case they doubt this miraculous transformation, God announces them to heaven's High Council with these words: "You are my witnesses" (Isa 43:12).

At the beginning of Acts, Jesus commissions his embryonic church to proclaim that in his life, death and resurrection a new and final exodus has taken place. "… and you will be my witnesses in Jerusalem, and in all Judea and Samaria, and to the ends of the earth" (Acts 1:8). We are the church of Jesus. We are the community that God called to explain and expound his big story to the world.

It remains one of the distinguishing points of the Christian revelation that Jesus did not write an autobiography or even dictate one. As the Father entrusted his words to Israel, so the Son has commissioned his church to share his good news. He has entrusted us not just to tell life-giving story but to become it. We are to embody his hope for the world as a living demonstration of new creation. We are God's tomorrow in the world today.

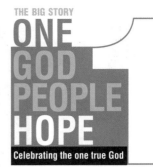

Recommended Reading

A Shorter Read

What Are We Waiting For?

Leading theologians and Christian thinkers discuss the issue of hope as it relates to theology, the Bible, the church and culture. The essays aim to provide a short and informative read.

"Isaiah" by John Goldingay

Provides a whistlestop tour through the eschatology of Isaiah.

A Longer Read

Joining God's Conspiracy by Tom Sine

Drawing together a theology of hope, analysis of current trends and stories from the emerging church, this book invites us all to join God's hopeful conspiracy with and for the world.

A Lighter Read

A Terrible Beauty by Chick Yuill

Challenges us to acknowledge the fierce splendour that is shot through human experience, that is most sharply focussed at Calvary, and that we must encounter and even embrace if we are to experience life in all its fullness.

The Heavenly Party by Michele Guinness (Monarch Books 2007)

Material from Jewish and other traditions has been given a messianic modification, imbuing it with rich and relevant celebration. Faith does not need to be dull, so start practicing now for the eternal party.

A Deeper Read

Hopeful Imagination: Prophetic Voices in Exit by Walter Brueggemann (Augsburg Fortress 1986)

Tracing the prophetic tradition through the Bible, provides an inspirational account of the history of God's hope.

A Book for all the Family

Telling the Bible: Over 100 Stories to Read Out Loud
by Bob Hartman (Monarch Books 2007)

A wonderful way for adults and children to enjoy and discover the Bible's most gripping stories, all retold by a master storyteller. This book is a rich resource, opening up new perspectives on familiar truths and bringing Scripture to life.

Resources for Churches

Mission of God: Exodus by Jenny Baker

This Spring Harvest Bible Workbook enables small groups to journey through the story of the Exodus and consider the implications for their own Christian pilgrimage.

5 ONE HOPE IN THE CITY

Hope in the city

Introduction

The final stage in our journey through God's big story is a look at the hope that is bigger than history, the end of this world and the final consummation of God's plan. We shall focus on three areas.

1. ISAIAH: Chapter 55 is a poetic rendition of Israel's future.

2. REVELATION: Isaiah's poetry is used to articulate a vision of the end.

3. THE CHURCH: As we grasp God's tomorrow, we change our today. The church can provide a taste of new creation.

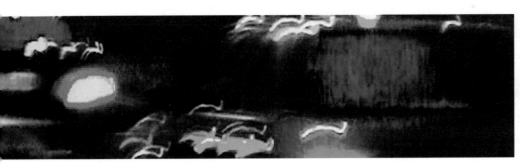

THE BIG STORY

ONE
GOD
PEOPLE
HOPE

Celebrating the one true God

1

Teaching Block 1:

Happily Ever After?

We begin with three accounts of God's plan for human history.

- Israel's happy ending and Isaiah's imaginative prophecy of the exiles' homecoming.
- John's apocalyptic vision in the book of Revelation and its prophetic importance for the early church.
- The church's call to be a prophetic signpost to God's hope for tomorrow.

Teaching Block 2:

At the End of the Day

We will address three end times themes from the big story.

- Judgment and salvation. What does it mean to call Christ the judge and saviour of creation?
- Hell and heaven. What does Scripture say about the consequences of God's final acts of judgment and salvation?
- The great banquet. Is it possible to understand and experience God's eternal future and offer it to the world?

Teaching Block 1:

> "From now on I will tell you of new things, of hidden things unknown to you. They are created now, and not long ago; you have not heard of them before today. So you cannot say, 'Yes, I knew of them.'"
>
> Isaiah 48:6ᵇ–7

Comment: "The Old Testament speaks very seldom about the end times … the Old Testament envisions the 'end' as taking place *within history* and within the framework of earthly Israel and its religion. Ancient Israel envisioned a future that was fundamentally *different* from and *better* than the present. It was improved beyond what could be expected from human progress… . Eschatology in the Old Testament portrays the *ideal* future … brought about by God."

Lena-Sofia Tiemeyer, "Eschatology in the Old Testament" in Stephen Holmes & Russell Rook (eds.), *What Are We Waiting For?* (Paternoster Press, Milton Keynes, 2008)

> "Come, all you who are thirsty, come to the waters; and you who have no money, come, buy and eat! Come, buy wine and milk without money and without cost. Why spend money on what is not bread, and your labour on what does not satisfy?"
>
> Isaiah 55:1–2ᵃ

Happily ever after?

1.1
Isaiah: adventures in the impossible

Israel's happy ending is laid out in Isaiah 55, which describes the great homecoming that awaits God's people in the new Jerusalem. However, many of the exiles had never seen the old Jerusalem so Isaiah's poetry was pushed to its limits trying to portray God's hope to his people.

This reveals the secret of prophecy. When we explain things we can often choose between explaining what actually happened and our experience of what happened. In describing the perfect future both modes fall short, so Isaiah engages his *imagination*. In effect, God's Spirit stretches the imagination of both prophet and audience to encompass the mysteries of heaven.

Chapter 55 projects a majestic scene; part market, part feast. The poetry assaults our senses and draws us toward the babble of a banquet. We're invited to join. It doesn't matter that we have no money, for here we can 'buy' food and drink for free. Isaiah makes no sense. If no money changes hands, then how are we buying anything? It is surely a give-away. But Isaiah makes the point three times that those with no money can buy the goods on offer. This prophecy is pushing the logic of language to its limits.

Over the last few days we have seen a persistent tension between God's sovereignty and our responsibility. Though it is ultimately his business, God makes the kingdom our business. It is as if we have gone to a grand banquet with a ticket that God bought for us, and on arrival we discover that we are not just guests but we will be contributing too.

Not only will the exiles return to Jerusalem, but so will foreigners. Not to invade or pillage Israel this time, but to join a party of praise to God. Nations will trade

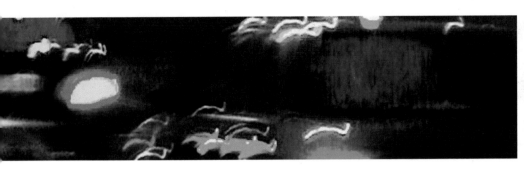

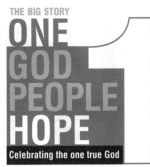

Hope Quote:

Imagination

Imagination is essential to Christian believing and living, and to Christian theology. … The way in which God makes himself known to us, and shares his redemptive purposes and promises for the world with us, is bound up with our capacity to imagine. Faith depends upon our apprehending and holding in our 'mind's eye' … things which trespass far beyond the horizons of the things we can see and touch and hear.

Trevor Hart, "Seeing visions and dreaming dreams," *What are we waiting for?*

Hope in Verse:

My happy home

Hierusalem, my happy home,
When shall I come to thee?
When shall my sorrows have an end,
Thy joys when shall I see?

O happy harbour of the saints,
O sweet and pleasant soil,
In thee no sorrow may be found
No grief, no care, no toil…

No dampish mist is seen in thee,
Nor cold nor darksome night;
There every soul shines as the sun,
There God himself gives light.

Anon.

Songs of Hope:

Study war no more

I'm gonna lay down my gun and belt
Down by the riverside
Down by the riverside
Down by the riverside
I'm gonna lay down my gun and belt
Down by the riverside
Ain't gonna study war no more

American Spiritual

space for notes

> "Listen, listen to me, and eat what is good, and your soul will delight in the richest of fare. Give ear and come to me; hear me, that your soul may live."
>
> Isaiah 55:2b–3a

> The revelation of Jesus Christ, which God gave him to show his servants what must soon take place.
>
> Revelation 1:1

> Then I heard every creature in heaven and on earth and under the earth and on the sea, and all that is in them, singing: "To him who sits on the throne and to the Lamb be praise and honour and glory and power, for ever and ever!"
>
> Revelation 5:13

their weapons for farm implements so that they can contribute to the heavenly banquet. God has to stretch their faith if Israel is to believe so he says, "My thoughts are not your thoughts." His hope for his people is by its nature beyond imagination, but by attending to these words we glimpse the new creation and hear the excited babble of an eternal banquet.

1.2 Revelation: in heaven's name, what's going on?

Over 500 years after the return from exile, John writes the book of Revelation. The title comes from the first verse, which says the book is "the revelation of Jesus Christ." The Greek word for revelation is *apokalypsis*.

Revelation is unlike any other book in the New Testament, which is why there are some difficulties interpreting it. The author was caught in the now and not yet of God's kingdom. Many of his contemporaries believed the second coming was imminent, some were persecuted and others questioned the delay in Jesus' return. Revelation's visual imagery stretches the reader's imagination and encourages believers to keep hoping in Christ.

Stylistically, it has a lot in common with other apocalypses such as Daniel. Like Isaiah, Revelation begins at the throne in heaven. God reveals a series of mysteries, assuring the church that he will rule history, aid his people and achieve his purposes. Isaiah provides the imaginative language for John to describe the final scenes of God's big story. The vision of Christ and the encouraging challenge for the church is the climax of the New Testament.

The book has three functions – prophecy, revelation and circular. The coming of God's kingdom is the grand theme of Scripture, and John understands Old Testament prophecy in this light. In Jesus the fulfilment of prophecy has begun.

John challenges the church to adopt heaven's perspective so it can see that, for instance, the world is not ruled by the Roman emperor. Since the law required everyone to hail the emperor as their lord and saviour, this was a revelation. John says the people, systems and ideas that claim to rule, order and govern society have no ultimate authority. True power and glory belong only to God. Anyone thinking we are ruled by kings, prime ministers, politics and a free market should take note, their claim to authority is as tenuous as was Caesar's.

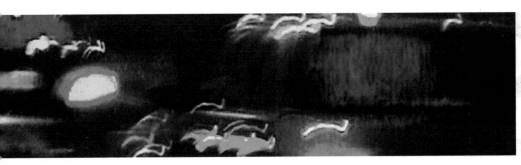

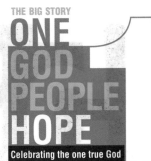

THE BIG STORY

ONE GOD PEOPLE HOPE

Celebrating the one true God

Hope Note:

Apocalyptic literature

"On the day after the deaths of thousands of people in the World Trade Center in New York City, a British tabloid newspaper had a single caption to accompany its terrible picture: 'APOCALYPSE'. One word was considered sufficient to epitomize the destruction," Judith Kovacs and Christopher Rowland write in *Revelation Through the Centuries*.

Biblical words often find themselves in headlines, so it is worth defining what theologians mean by 'apocalypse'. *The Open Heaven* by Christopher Rowland outlines the main ingredients of Jewish and early Christian apocalyptic literature. This distinct brand of prophecy, it says, includes the following key elements:

• A DYNAMIC ENCOUNTER with God, often where the prophet ascends into heaven.

• A TESTIMONY that God does not stand by and watch history in the making but intervenes to bring about his own will and purpose.

• A PROCLAMATION that a new day is dawning.

• An ANNOUNCEMENT that God's chosen servant or messiah will bring in, or herald, a new age.

• A REVELATION of divine mysteries previously known only in the heavens.

• An EXPECTATION that the new era will vindicate those who believe in resurrection.

Although not all of Isaiah fits strictly into the category of apocalyptic, as you can see from the list above, it does feature many of the main categories that Rowland outlines.

Hope in Verse:

Time and eternity

I never saw a moor,
I never saw the sea;
Yet know I how the heather looks,
And what a wave must be.

I never spoke with God,
Nor visited in Heaven;
Yet certain am I of the spot
As if the chart were given.

Emily Dickinson (1830–1886)

5 ONE HOPE IN THE CITY

"He who overcomes will inherit all this, and I will be his God and he will be my son."

Revelation 21:7

Comment: "[Although Revelation] concerns the final victory of God's rule over all evil and the final completion of God's purpose in the new creation of all things, it portrays the coming of God's kingdom in direct relation to the situation of its first readers. The eschatological future is envisaged in terms of its impact on the present, so that the first readers might see how to live in their own situation in the light of the coming kingdom.... We need to bear in mind throughout both the original context to which it first spoke and the way it continues to illuminate the truth of new situations in the light of God's kingdom."

Richard Bauckham, "Eschatology in the Book of Revelation" in Stephen Holmes & Russell Rook (eds.), *What Are We Waiting For?* (Paternoster Press, Milton Keynes, 2008)

Then I saw a new heaven and a new earth, for the first heaven and the first earth had passed away, and there was no longer any sea. I saw the Holy City, the new Jerusalem, coming down out of heaven from God, prepared as a bride beautifully dressed for her husband. And I heard a loud voice from the throne saying, "Now the dwelling of God is with men, and he will live with them. They will be his people, and God himself will be with them and be their God. He will wipe every tear from their eyes. There will be no more death or mourning or crying or pain, for the old order of things has passed away."

Revelation 21:1–4

Revelation is addressed to seven churches, a number that denotes completeness and means it is a gift to the whole church. To make proper use of this gift in our own time it is essential that we familiarise ourselves with the context of the original audience. The symbols and signs of Revelation may be confusing to us, but they were familiar to people in the early church. As did Isaiah, John uses his imagination to convey truths far beyond everyday understanding.

Attempts to interpret Revelation literally are doomed for at least two reasons.

Firstly, it is possible to read countless current and historical events into Revelation. For centuries Christians have said it means the end of the world was near. Since we are here, it clearly wasn't near.

Secondly, the events within Revelation are not in date order. For instance, having been flattened by an earthquake in chapter sixteen, Babylon falls again in chapters seventeen, eighteen and nineteen. While it is undoubtedly prophetic, Revelation is not a prediction of specific events. Attempts to use it as an end times wall planner are ill-advised.

John's first priority in writing Revelation was to help Christians come to terms with their part in God's big story. He uses Old Testament imagery in his descriptions of plagues, trumpets, lamp-stands, bowls and scrolls. He reassures those who long for Christ's return that Jesus will win the day and his followers are on the winning team. They will inherit the splendour of the new Jerusalem, and victory is both imminent and immanent. By trusting in his victorious future, God's people become winners in the present.

Having begun with heaven and earth divided, John's vision closes with the two united. The new heaven and the new earth will become one, and the new Jerusalem will be the capital. This happy ending will come about through Christ. He is the first and the last, the Lamb who sits upon the throne, the king of perfected creation. It will also come about through the faithful witness of his followers, who will inevitably suffer pain, persecution and even martyrdom.

Near the end of the war, the Lamb's followers appear utterly overwhelmed by three ghastly monsters. A violent beast seems to have secured the worship of the world, yet as with the Easter story he is overcome by the faithfulness of God's persecuted church. The true victors are the martyrs, those who have followed the example of their master to the end. Their witness is a moment of divine illumination in which God's truth exposes the lies of the beast and Christ's suffering servants save the world.

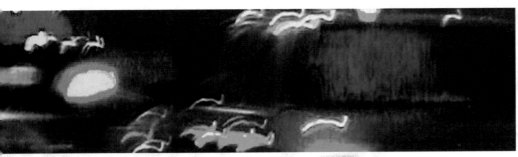

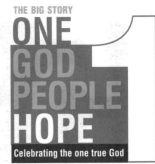

Hope Quote:

Predicting the future

Unfortunately, the book of Revelation is probably best known as a happy hunting-ground for millenarian enthusiasts who find the events of their own time plotted in marvellous detail in its prophecies and can thereby predict the precise course of future events up to and including the rapture, the Second Coming, and the millennium. In the United States, in particular, this kind of interpretation is as popular as it ever was, perhaps more so. But similar kinds of interpretation – identifying current events as specific fulfilments of Revelation's prophecies and thereby conclud-ing that the final events of history are soon to come – have flourished in most periods and places of Christian history. The sheer variety of such readings down the centuries should make one cautious of supposing that now, at last, we can get it right. Is this kind of prediction really what the book is for?

Richard Bauckham, "Eschatology in the Book of Revelation," *What Are We Waiting For?*

Hope Quote:

Heaven not my home

Christians regularly speak of their hope in terms of 'going to heaven when they die'. One hears it in hymns … in prayers. The point seems to be that there is something called 'eternity', which is regularly spoken of as though it has only the loosest of connections with space and time, and one day we are going to step into this eternal existence, … which has almost nothing to do with this earth and this present history. … I suggest instead that what we find in the New Testament … is the Christian hope for a new, or renewed, heaven and a new, or renewed earth, with these two integrated together.

Tom Wright, *New Heavens, New Earth*

Hope Quote:

The time and the date

When I first became a Christian, I thought I knew everything. I even thought I knew when the world would end. After all, I had bought an *End of the World Wall Planner* from the bearded lady at my local Christian book shop.

Jeff Lucas

Hope in Verse:

St Cecilia's Day 1687

So when the last and dreadful hour
This crumbling pageant shall devour,
The trumpet shall be heard on high,
The dead shall live, the living die,
And music shall untune the sky!

John Dryden (1639–1701)

5 ONE HOPE IN THE CITY

John reveals the secret of a victorious Christian. Christians do not rise above every trial, cure every ill, heal every sickness or win every battle. They suffer and wonder why. They fight and find themselves losing. They pursue powerlessness rather than power. They seek servanthood rather than high status. They gain victory by sacrifice, not savagery. And unlikely though it may seem, they win the world for God.

We can take great encouragement from this. It is in the daily grind of faithful living that we contribute to God's plans for creation. Moments when we appear outnumbered or outmanoeuvred will be transformed into cosmic victories as we defeat the enemy by the power of our testimony and the blood of the Lamb.

The last part of John's vision concerns the outcome of this war. The corrupt city of Babylon is replaced by a new Jerusalem. All of God's promises are fulfilled and creation is transformed by God's immediate presence. The new Jerusalem is Eden perfected. The story that began in a garden ends in a city.

Revelation ends with the Holy Spirit and the church speaking with one voice. The words are familiar but the image is startling. By the power of his Spirit and in the lives of his people, God's message to Isaiah is fulfilled. Christ's followers invite others to the banquet who then contribute by joining the chorus. In the power of the Spirit, they also invite creation to join the banquet. Everything is prepared for the guest of honour. Christ has invited us to pray for his coming, and so we say, Come, Lord Jesus.

> The Spirit and the bride say, "Come!"
> And let him who hears say, "Come!"
> Whoever is thirsty, let him come; and whoever wishes, let him take the free gift of the water of life.
>
> Revelation 22:17

1.3
Apocalypse now

Isaiah and Revelation are not diaries of the end times but handbooks on the exciting challenge of living a prophetic life. While neither Isaiah nor John saw the end of history, both lived through climactic moments. They span a period covering life in the promised land, the invasion of Jerusalem by Nebuchadnezzar, exile in Babylon, a great homecoming, the rise and fall of regimes, the coming of Jesus, and the fall of the Roman Empire. Each of these events radically altered the world in one way or another, marking the end of the world as people knew it. One era ended, another began, and God's word was always there so his people would know their part in the next chapter of his story.

We may not witness the second coming, but we are seeing the transformation of the world. Recent times have seen two world wars, the rise and fall

THE BIG STORY
ONE
GOD
PEOPLE
HOPE
Celebrating the one true God

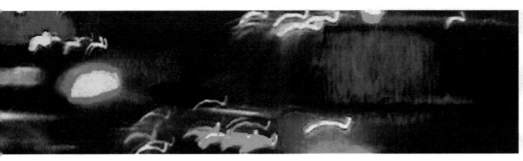

Hope Quote:

Bad world

This is a cheerful world as I see it from my garden under the shadows of my vines. But if I were to ascend some high mountain and look out over the wide lands, you know very well what I would see: brigands on the highways, pirates on the sea, armies fighting, cities burning; in the amphitheatres men murdered to please applauding crowds; selfishness and cruelty and misery and despair under all roofs.

It is a bad world, Donatus, an incredibly bad world. But I have discovered in the midst of it a quiet and holy people who have learned a great secret. They have found a joy which is a thousand times better than any pleasure of sinful life. They are despised and persecuted, but they care not. They are masters of their souls. They have overcome the world. These people, Donatus, are the Christians, and I am one of them.

Cyprian, bishop of Carthage (AD250)

Story of Hope:

They will overcome

In *No Future Without Forgiveness*, his account of the South African Truth and Reconciliation Commission, Archbishop Desmond Tutu describes how those who had been oppressed and marginalized by generations of apartheid finally overcame this demonic system of rule. The bloody revolution predicted by many never arrived, thanks in large part to the faithful prayers and powerful grace of God's people. Tutu's description of the nation's first general election provides a contemporary parallel to the book of Revelation.

"Everywhere else elections are secular political events. Ours was more than this, much, much more. It was a veritable spiritual experience, a mountain-top experience. The black person entered the booth one person and emerged on the other side a new, transfigured one. She entered weighed down by the anguish and burden of oppression, with the memory of being treated like rubbish gnawing away at her like some corrosive acid. She reappeared knowing she was free, walking away with her head held high, shoulders set straighter and an elastic spring in her step. How do you convey that sense of freedom which tastes like sweet nectar the first time you experience it? How do you describe it to someone who was born into freedom? ...It is a feeling that makes you want to laugh and cry, to dance with joy and yet at the same time you fear that it is too good to be true and that it just might all evaporate."

Desmond Tutu, *No Future Without Forgiveness*

5 ONE HOPE IN THE CITY

of Communism, the start and end of the cold war, Third World debt, a communications revolution, the birth of a climate crisis and globalisation. With each momentous event a part of the world ended and another began, impacting lives in profound ways. Relationships, family life, callings, communities, lifestyles, livelihood, work-life balance and ways of doing church have all been affected by the changes in the world.

Isaiah and Revelation teach us not to be surprised by wars and rumours of wars, but to see history with heaven's eyes and acknowledge God's coming kingdom. We have to go beyond intellectual assent and live as though his kingdom had already come, subjecting every aspect of our lives to his rule. We are God's people, and God's people are citizens of heaven. We cannot escape the troublesome, and often painful, realities of history but we can point out that it won't be like this forever. We can show people what the coming kingdom will be like through the distinctive way we live out God's story.

In some ways the world hasn't changed much since life in ancient Babylon and Rome. Plenty of rulers, governments, systems and philosophies still claim absolute authority. Free market economies rule much of the world. Money is everyone's business. The rich get richer and the poor get poorer. The pattern goes unchecked. The question remains unasked.

Christians know that the future does not belong to those who control the global stock markets. The God who rules history does economics differently, inviting the world to a banquet it doesn't deserve, holding a market of the finest of fare where he doesn't charge a penny.

Most of us don't understand the FTSE 100 share index or worship money, but we are competing in a race to buy the most toys before we die. The contest for a bigger house, faster car and nicer holiday is often deciding our future for us. Every aspect of our life has a price tag pinned to it, even time. To get more money, we cram as much work as possible into each week. How else can we afford our mortgage? Our attempts to escape the rat race appear certain to fail. We watch television to relax, only to be told to redesign our homes, refill our wardrobes, re-mortgage our houses and rejoin the rat race.

Christians worship Jesus, the beginning and end of all things. Christians have nothing to fear in living differently – work less, give more, live in a deprived area, volunteer – but it takes enormous willpower. The nuts and bolts of discipleship are the daily decisions we make to worship Jesus by living differently. The details of our lives identify what god we serve, the small things declare

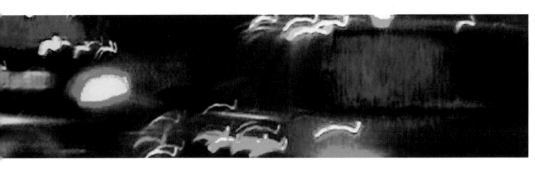

Hope Quote:

Kingdom come

Revelation's purpose is to enable its readers to continue to pray and to live Jesus' prayer: 'Your kingdom come.'

Richard Bauckham, "Eschatology in the Book of Revelation", *What Are We Waiting For?*

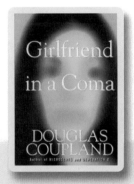

Story of Hope:

Modern day apocalypse

Girlfriend in a Coma (1998) took the sense of spiritual longing of [Douglas] Coupland's earlier work and invested it with a sense of urgency. It asks big questions about value, holiness and faith. Do we expect to be judged? Is there any hope of redemption? Christians often assume that these kinds of question are only asked in very specific church contexts… But *Girlfriend in a Coma* is proof that these issues are articulated in unexpected places and often more imaginatively than we anticipate too. Unlike many 'official', sanctioned religious writers, Coupland is wrestling with the truth in all its messiness. It might not be comfortable but it's probably a lot closer to the truth, and to the kind of images of faith offered in the Bible, as a result… .

The eponymous heroine of the novel wakes up after a 17-year coma to discover that her once idealistic friends have simply given up on life. They've slipped into a whole range of addictions (including work and greed as well as the more obvious narcotic dependencies). However, there is still hope. Hope is the emotion that makes Coupland's fiction distinctive … from his peers. One character reassures his friends that the possibility of holiness and, ultimately, of redemption hasn't just evaporated. However, redemption is also presented as something that is lived out in the dangerous space of questions, quest and pilgrimage. The after-life is depicted as a blinding reality that is too much for humanity, this side of heaven, to bear but which needs to be believed to be seen.

The end of *Girlfriend in a Coma* made lots of critics very uneasy because it seemed to demand a thorough re-evaluation of the way in which its characters live. He isn't a straightforwardly political or religious writer in the ordinary sense. Yet his fiction always suggests that a greater reality than the one that consumer culture demands that we buy into exists. He doesn't offer a weird, homespun philosophy and I suspect that he'd hate the idea of being labelled a prophet. But, for my money, his writing is bursting with a sense of the transcendent that is found amidst the everyday and with a belief that the pursuit of meaning and what Christians regard as the sacred, is infinitely valuable.

Andrew Tate, *Douglas Coupland*
(Manchester University Press 2007)

Accessories – scarves, hats

Clothes

Jewellery/Makeup

Mobile phone / MP3 / gadgets

Shoes

How much are you carrying?

Using the models as representative of yourself, write in each box an approximate value of everything you are wearing or carrying on your person.

Add these boxes together and put the total in the final box. If you could write a cheque out for that amount today, who would you send it to and why?

How many countries were involved in the manufacture of everything you are carrying?

Total value of items worn

where our hope lies – in Caesar, the gods of Babylon, the global economy, or the one true God.

Revelation shows God's people worshipping a lamb that is on a throne. It's a strange, even surreal, image, but it illustrates the upside-down nature of Christ's kingdom. A person who claims to have power will one day be powerless, while a person who gives up power will be powerful. As painful and challenging as it might be to uncover what god we are serving, the promised end is freedom.

Rejecting what the world says, the big story says that those who give will get, those who place themselves last will come first, and those who appear powerless will know the power behind heaven's throne. If we give and place ourself last we will take our part in God's story. What's more, we will demonstrate God's kingdom. He is the real king and this is what the end of history will really look like.

Teaching Block 2:

At the end of the day

2.1
Judgment and salvation

While salvation is the great hope of the Christian faith, it assumes some notion of judgment. Contemporary thought tends to treat judgment and salvation as opposites, saying a kind god saves and an angry god judges. The fact that God is both saviour and judge leads some people to diagnose multiple personality disorder where he alternates between New Testament God, who is gentle Jesus meek and mild, and Old Testament God, who is jealous and vengeful. We need to reconcile the two.

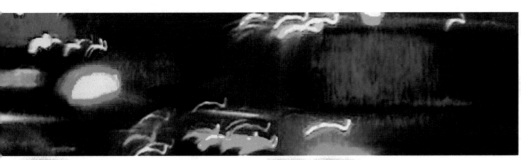

THE BIG STORY

ONE 1
GOD
PEOPLE
HOPE
Celebrating the one true God

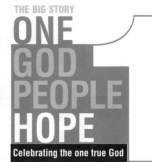

Story of Hope:

From horror to hope

In the afterword to her novel *Christ the Lord*, Anne Rice relates how detailed historical research into the world in which Christ lived led to her return to faith. In her tale about the childhood and self-discovery of Jesus, the author of *Vampire Chronicles* and *Interview with the Vampire* pays meticulous attention to the cultural and historical backdrop to Christ's life. Though obviously a work of fiction, the detailed setting provides a remarkable account of first century Palestinian life. Rice explains.

"As I sat on the floor of my office surrounded by books about Sumer, Egypt, Rome, etc., and some sceptical material about Jesus that had come into my hands, I couldn't understand how the [Jews had endured] as the great people who they were.

"It was this that drew me back to God. It set in motion the idea that there may in fact be God. And when that hap-pened there grew in me for whatever reason an immense desire to return to the banquet table. In 1998 I went back to the Catholic church.

"But even then I had not closed in on the question of Jesus Christ and Christianity. … In 2002 I put aside everything else and decided to focus entirely on answering the questions that had dogged me all my life. The decision came in July of that year. I had been reading the Bible constantly,… and I decided that I would give myself utterly to the task of trying to understand Jesus himself and how Christianity emerged.

"I wanted to write the life of Christ. I had known that years ago. But now I was ready. I was ready to do violence to my career. … I consecrated the book to Christ. I consecrated myself and my work to Christ."

Hope Quote:

Nasty person

The God of the Old Testament is arguably the most unpleasant character in all fiction.

Richard Dawkins, *The God Delusion*, 31

Hope in Verse:

Love and justice

One of the most famous and influential accounts of God's judgement undoubtedly belongs to Dante. Brian Horne says we can learn from the great poet's depiction of divine judgement.

"By the end of Dante's journey, he has learnt that love governs the whole universe. Love even governs inferno. And that is the astonishing thing – that justice and love aren't separable. That to love means to be just and to be just means to love. One of the great insights of medieval Catholic theology is the bringing together of justice and love like this. Love is not some kind of mushy sentiment – it is something which entails the just operation of the universe.

"Love is at the centre of inferno wrapped up in the idea of perfect justice. Right over the terrible gates are the words: 'Love was my maker.'"

5 ONE HOPE IN THE CITY

Strengthen the feeble hands, steady the knees that give way; say to those with fearful hearts, "Be strong, do not fear; your God will come, he will come with vengeance; with divine retribution he will come to save you."

Isaiah 35:3–4

The earth dries up and withers, the world languishes and withers, the exalted of the earth languish. The earth is defiled by its people; they have disobeyed the laws, violated the statutes, and broken the everlasting covenant. Therefore a curse consumes the earth; its people must bear their guilt.

Isaiah 24:4–6ᵃ

Comment: As in Revelation, the Old Testament uses images like the serpent, the sea monster and the dragon to personify the power of sin upon the earth.

Let the wicked forsake his way and the evil man his thoughts. Let him turn to the LORD, and he will have mercy on him, and to our God, for he will freely pardon. "For my thoughts are not your thoughts, neither are your ways my ways," declares the LORD.

Isaiah 55:7–8

In Isaiah, God performs miraculous saving acts and frightening acts of judgment yet the prophet never treats him as fickle or erratic. For Isaiah sees God's ministries of salvation and judgment as necessarily one and the same. Because God has perfect judgment, he makes the perfect saviour; because God is the perfect saviour, he is also the perfect judge.

So the exile was not caused by a break in God's faithfulness. In fact, the exact opposite is true. It was Israel's faithlessness that caused her hopelessness. God hoped Israel would care for the widow and orphan, worship no other God and be a light to the Gentiles. But Israel rejected God's hope, negating her calling as his people and forsaking her birthright. Israel chose to become something other than God's chosen nation.

God periodically warned Israel, as Isaiah reminds us, where her neglect of God's calling would lead. If Israel had heeded God's judgment she would have been spared the pain of exile. Although Israel has to experience the consequences of her apathy, God's perfect judgment means she will not suffer indefinitely. Isaiah 55 is a picture of hope, showing where Israel's journey will lead. Not to expiration in Babylon but to a homecoming party in the new Jerusalem.

Isaiah and John both view the world as being caught up in a cosmic conflict. While God remains sovereign, he stays above the skirmishes and does not always assert this sovereignty. He allows his purposes to be frustrated by the free will of his people. However, God will one day kill Leviathan the gliding serpent, the embodiment of evil and sin.

In the New Testament, the cosmic conflict is won by Jesus as God's salvation and justice come together on the cross. God does not exercise justice solely by warning us of the consequences of our actions, and he gets no enjoyment from the horrors of judgment. God experiences the full force of justice, paying the wages of his people's sins and suffering the consequences of their hopeless actions, through Jesus. The divine sacrifice defeats the forces of darkness and demonstrates the perfect way in which God saves and judges the world.

As the creator of the beginning and the ends of the earth, God is both the world's judge and its saviour. We can speculate as to the nature of his judgment, but all we know is that God will do it to perfection for he alone has earned the right to judge and save the world. The one who hosts the heavenly banquet is the first and last of all creation, the sacrificial lamb who sits upon the throne.

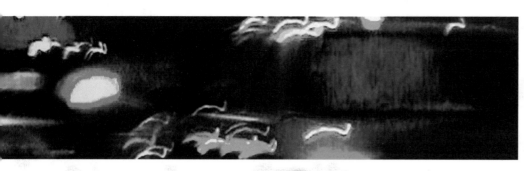

Story of Hope:

The final judgment

At the end of time, billions of people were seated on a great plain before God's throne. Most shrank back from the brilliant light before them. But some groups near the front talked heatedly, not cringing with cringing shame – but with belligerence.

"Can God judge us? How can he know about suffering?" snapped a young woman. She ripped open a sleeve to reveal a tattooed number from a Nazi concentration camp. "We endured terror ... beatings ... torture ... death!"

In another group a boy lowered his collar. "What about this?" he demanded, showing an ugly rope burn. "Lynched, for no crime but being black!"

In another crowd there was a pregnant schoolgirl with sullen eyes: "Why should I suffer?" she murmured. "It wasn't my fault." Far out across the plain were hundreds of such groups. Each had a complaint against God for the evil and suffering he had permitted in his world.

How lucky God was to live in heaven, where all was sweetness and light. Where there was no weeping or fear, no hunger or hatred. What did God know of all that man had been forced to endure in this world? For God leads a pretty sheltered life, they said.

So each of these groups sent forth their leader, chosen because he had suffered the most. A Jew, an African, a person from Hiroshima, a horribly deformed arthritic, a child born with HIV. In the centre of the vast plain, they consulted with each other. At last they were ready to present their case. It was rather clever.

Before God could be qualified to be their judge, he must endure what they had endured. Their decision was that God should be sentenced to live on earth as a man.

Let him be born a Jew. Let the legitimacy of his birth be doubted. Give him a work so difficult that even his family will think him out of his mind.

Let him be betrayed by his closest friends. Let him face false charges, be tried by a prejudiced jury and convicted by a cowardly judge. Let him be tortured.

At the last, let him see what it means to be terribly alone. Then let him die so there can be no doubt he died. Let there be a great host of witnesses to verify it.

As each leader announced his portion of the sentence, loud murmurs of approval went up from the throng of people assembled. When the last had finished pronouncing sentence, there was a long silence. No one uttered a word. No one moved.

For suddenly, all knew that God had already served his sentence.

Russell Rook, adapted from Anon, *The Long Silence*, http://www.ldolphin.org/silence.html (a version of this story is attributed to ATL Armstrong in David Self, *One Hundred Readings for Assembly*, Harcourt Heinemann 1993)

5 ONE HOPE IN THE CITY

2.2
Hell and heaven

Isaiah and Revelation both look towards God's full and final judgment of all things. And both raise the question of how life will look after final judgment. The big story does not simply look to the end of human history but beyond this to a new eternal history. What can we really say about this new reality? In the church this discussion has revolved around the doctrines of heaven and hell, so in this section we will outline some of the ways in which Christians have understood these doctrines.

Hope in hell?

The idea of hell is obviously unattractive, and the doctrine is often unpopular. The concept of hell retains currency mostly in the realm of fantasy, for instance horror movies, gothic novels and certain genres of popular music, and it remains a useful metaphor. "I've had a hell of a day," we sometimes say. Or, "That experience was hellish." Outside these narrow areas people often find the concept difficult and try to avoid it.

Three main views of hell occur within Christian tradition.

Eternal Conscious Torment is what many regard as the classic version of this doctrine. The horror of this hell is its unremitting eternity, with no day or night. As all sins are an offence against the eternal God, it states, and they carry eternal consequences. In Revelation, John writes of the beast who will suffer torment forever; the beast refers to Nero, a Roman emperor who demanded the worship of his subjects and persecuted Christians for not participating. It is hardly surprising that John reserves such a damning judgment for him. The arguments against eternal conscious torment revolve around alternative ways of reading the biblical texts. To punish people eternally for a momentary sin, many argue, runs contrary to God's good nature.

Annihilation is the main alternative in Evangelical circles. According to this view the punishment of hell is the end of existence. It argues that the Bible speaks of eternal consequences of God's judgment not an eternal state of judgment. Fire is a metaphor implying that in God's judgment sinners will be destroyed and consumed rather than remaining conscious for eternity. Revelation, for instance, says that those omitted from the book of life are thrown into the fire. Annihilationists still believe in an eternal hell since non-existence is an eternal state. Furthermore, they claim that eternal life is a gift from God through the work of his saving grace. Without this gift, human beings are mortal and death

> "And the smoke of their torment rises for ever and ever. There is no rest day or night for those who worship the beast and his image, or for anyone who receives the mark of his name".
> Revelation 14:11

> If anyone's name was not found in the book of life, he was thrown into the lake of fire.
> Revelation 20:15

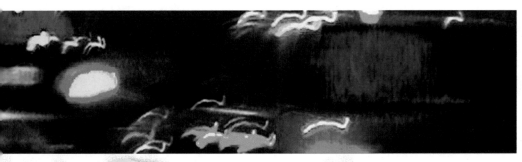

THE BIG STORY

ONE
GOD
PEOPLE
HOPE

1

Celebrating the one true God

Dante's inferno

Brian Horne describes the hopelessness of Dante's hell.

"Those in hell are those who have lost the capacity to love. There is absolute hopelessness and over the portals of hell are some of the most terrible words:

'Through me you enter the woeful city
Through me, you enter eternal grief
Through me, you enter among the lost
Abandon all hope you who enter here.'

"In hell, you enter the sphere of those who have lost hope. Not in a sad kind of way, they aren't longing for something they can't get – they don't even know what they want they have become so identified with their sins and crimes and there's no future, except the eternal present of lost-ness."

Supernatural stories

Graphic novels use the language of the supernatural realms to tell their stories. The DC/Vertigo comic book *Hellblazer* is the story of a man whose 'gift' is being able to see demons and angels. The film adaptation – *Constantine* (2005) – has the tagline "Hell wants him. Heaven won't take him. Earth needs him." It is a story rooted in theological concepts, but with a warped perspective.

Hellboy (2004) , another comic and film adaptation, is the story of a demon who grows up to defend humans against the forces of darkness.

The story lines in graphic novels are just one area where we find a widening collection of pluralistic views of the supernatural. Christians must ensure they are not ignorant or dismissive of these conflicting and creative takes on truth, but ready to engage in meaningful conversation with them no matter how far-fetched they seem.

Vision of hell

What will hell be like? … The pains of hell will be retributive and utterly just – they will involve evildoers being paid back for the wrongs they have done. … Hell will be final; those who go there will have no opportunities to turn back the clock and repent. Hell will include the "hell" of utter and endless regret, remorse and despair.

Mark R. Talbot, "Hell: A Horror Beyond Imagining"
Decision Magazine (May 2007)
http://www.billygraham.org/
DMag_article.asp?ArticleID=824

Annihilation, please

Emotionally, I find the concept [of eternal torment] intolerable and do not understand how people can live with it without either cauterizing their feelings or cracking under the strain. But our emotions are a fluctuating, unreliable guide to truth and must not be exalted to the place of supreme authority in determining it. As a committed Evangelical, my question must be—and is—not what my heart tells me, but what does God's word say? And in order to answer this question, we need to survey the biblical material afresh and to open our minds (not just our hearts) to the possibility that Scripture points in the direction of annihilationism, and that 'eternal conscious torment' is a tradition which has to yield to the supreme authority of Scripture.

John Stott in John Stott and David L. Edwards, *Essentials: A Liberal-Evangelical Dialogue* (London, 1988)

space for notes

"All nations will come and worship before you, for your righteous acts have been revealed."

Revelation 15:4[b]

The nations will walk by its light, and the kings of the earth will bring their splendour into it.

Revelation 21:24

Comment: Some scholars interpret the final judgment in Revelation as a final opportunity for all who have ever lived to view God in all his glory and to worship him. In this way, every knee may bow and every tongue confess that Jesus Christ is Lord to the glory of God the Father.

"I will rejoice over Jerusalem and take delight in my people."

Isaiah 65:19

"I did not see a temple in the city, because the Lord God Almighty and the Lamb are its temple."

Revelation 21:22

They will see his face, and his name will be on their foreheads. There will be no more night. They will not need the light of a lamp or the light of the sun, for the Lord God will give them light. And they will reign for ever and ever.

Revelation 22:4

Comment: "[John's vision] is actually a uniting of heaven and earth into a new creation. In this vision the dwelling place of God and the dwelling place of humanity become one new 'city', one new integrated creation in which God and humanity in all its fullness find a new eternal home."

Darrell Cosden, "Eschatology goes to Work" in Stephen Holmes & Russell Rook (eds.), *What Are We Waiting For?* (Paternoster Press, Milton Keynes, 2008)

After this I looked and there before me was a great multitude that no-one could count, from every nation, tribe, people and language, standing before the throne and in front of the Lamb.

Revelation 7:9

is their God-given end. The arguments against annihilation concern other biblical passages.

Restorative Punishment is a less represented interpretation of hell that attempts to reconcile two seemingly contradictory themes of Scripture – all will be saved, and some will go to hell. Revelation shows all the nations basking in God's light in the new Jerusalem. And yet how can anyone not saved enjoy this eternity? The restorative punishment view says that God's judgment is not about retribution but restoration. It's how God refines and perfects people so that they can join him in eternity. This view is often favoured by *Universalists*, who assert that a perfect and all-powerful God of love is willing and able to save everyone.

All three interpretations of the doctrine of hell can be argued from the book of Revelation, so all three must be considered. The victims of the dramatic judgments in Isaiah and Revelation are sometimes unexpected, and may be those who worship God as much as those who oppose him. It's the same way with God's mercy and salvation. God invites all manner of people to his party.

Despite the different positions on hell, the implications of God's judgment and salvation are undeniably universal. What's more, the character of the decision maker is beyond question. God is the first and the last, the one who knows and understands all things and is qualified to make perfect judgments.

Hope in heaven

Whatever our view on hell, we can agree that heaven is preferred. Before proceeding, however, we must clarify that heaven as a place where we go to when we die is largely alien to the biblical accounts.

We understand heaven and earth as distinct parts of God's creation, but Isaiah and John point out that they are linked. The battles in the heavenly realms and the daily skirmishes on earth are intrinsically related. God's work of new creation continues in heaven and on earth and in the future, or God's time, there will be a new heaven and a new earth. They will join together in the new Jerusalem.

Inspired by Isaiah, John locates his happy ending in the holy city, the new Jerusalem, the capital of new creation, where God dwells with his people and all creation praises him together. There is no need for a temple as everyone enjoys the full force of God's omnipresence. They all experience Christ's humanity fully. Filled by his Spirit and freed from sin and death, we will know Jesus as our brother and God as our father. The purity and power of this relationship will

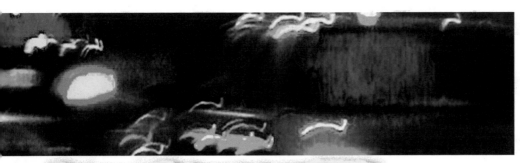

Hope Quote:

Universal truths?

At the most simple, the following two claims can be said to entail universalism. (1) God, being love, wants to save humanity. (2) God, being all powerful, can save all humanity. He wants to and he can so he will. The obvious objection is that whilst God may wish to save all and may be able to save all it is possible that the cost of his doing so may be unacceptable to him. One version of this response is the classic Arminian objection that saving all people would require God to over-ride freedom and that is unacceptable to him. If we choose to reject God forever then God will honour that choice. However, some Christian philosophers argue that God could save all people without violating human freewill. If such controversial claims are right then God could save everyone without undermining our freedom and so, according to the universalist, he would do so.

Robin Parry, "Hell: The Punishment of the Age
to Come," What are we waiting for?

Hope Quote:

Heaven

Heaven is the eternal increase of joy.

Questions of Hope:

Final act of love

Bill died three weeks ago, after a long illness. He was loved by his large family and respected as a great husband, father and grandfather. He rarely went to church and it is unlikely he had faith in God.

At his funeral service I did what I always do in such circumstances, I stated the hope in Christ that is available to all those who walk this earth; I spoke of the comfort that God offers and shared words of truth and comfort. I used familiar passages: "Jesus said to her, 'I am the resurrection and the life. He who believes in me will live, even though he dies." And also, "In my Father's house are many rooms; if it were not so, I would have told you. I am going there to prepare a place for you."

A funeral service is an opportunity to talk about the hope that is integral to the gospel and also a time to comfort those who grieve and mourn. It is a time to celebrate someone's life and to be grateful for all the good things that were shared and remembered but it is not a time to give false hope. It is not appropriate to talk about that person being with God when that seems unlikely.

At funerals for those whose faith is uncertain we can state the truth about the gospel hope and leave mourners to ask further or to draw their own conclusions if they wish. Gracious, gentle concern for the grieving is also part of the gospel message which must be expressed. Pastorally it is appropriate to comfort and support, to state the truth of the hope of Christian faith and not to judge.

Dianne Tidball
Regional Minister,
East Midlands Baptist Association

5 ONE HOPE IN THE CITY

space for notes

> "… the mountains and hills will burst into song before you, and all the trees of the field will clap their hands."
>
> Isaiah 55:12[b]

> He who was seated on the throne said, "I am making everything new! … It is done. I am the Alpha and the Omega, the Beginning and the End. To him who is thirsty I will give to drink without cost from the spring of the water of life."
>
> Revelation 21:5–6

extend to every aspect of life. We shall see the world as he does and know and love each other as he loves us.

If new creation occurs when history is complete, what happens to God's people until then? In short, where are our ancestors? Jews believe in a state called *sheol*, which is a sleep-like condition for the faithful until they rise on the day of resurrection. Over the years, Christian theologians have packaged numerous variations of this. Some proposed that Christ's resurrection made eternal life available now, so the new heaven and earth are already accessible to those in Christ. Others argued that because God holds the future the new heaven and the new earth already exist in him and so, although time is incomplete, the saints are with him today in paradise.

Many of the views proposed are not mutually exclusive. And they all hold one thing in common, our access to the new heaven and earth comes through the resurrection. This one event inaugurated God's new creation. The resurrected Jesus opened a door between the fallen and perfect worlds, between sin's imprisonment and eternal freedom. When we die we will leave unfinished history behind and enter God's eternity. The gateway to the new heaven and earth is already open now, we don't have to wait until the end of time, because Jesus has already risen from the dead. There is no significant gap between time and eternity.

Heaven is, by its nature, beyond us. However, the power of the resurrection makes it possible to speak of, and experience, new creation. The prophetic imaginings of Isaiah and John provide a foretaste of God's tomorrow in the midst of our today. We will pick out four examples.

1. **The future is a party**. Isaiah and Revelation both paint a picture of new creation as a party, a global reunion of all creation, in God's kingdom. As we pre-enact this party in our own communities, bringing together people of different cultures and backgrounds, we get a taste of the feast to come.

2. **The future is a family**. In new creation we will truly know, understand and love one another and God's world. As we attempt to imitate God's perfect love in our imperfect world, God's kingdom invades his world.

3. **The future is transformation**. While we will one day see him face to face, in Christ we have already encountered God. Having been transformed by this beatific vision it becomes possible to see God in others.

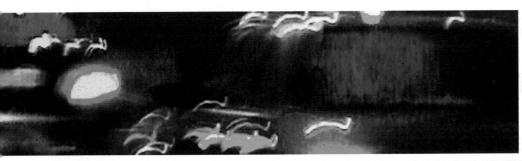

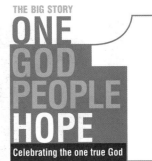

Hope Quote:

Recognition in heaven

Do you think that you will recognize me because you know me, and that you will not recognize my father whom you do not know? … You will know everybody. Those who will be there will not recognize each other because they will see their countenances; there will be mutual recognition because of greater knowledge. Thus, all will see and will see much more keenly. … When they will be filled with God, they will see divinely.

Augustine, *Sermons*, 243.6

Hope Note:

Worship/Service

A curious phrase that occurs in the middle of the wonderful vision of Revelation 22 proves particularly poignant at this point. Having spoken of the river of life, the throne of God and the Lamb, the glorious fruit and all that is there, we find this: "The throne of God and of the Lamb will be in the city, and his servants will serve him" (Rev 22:3). It echoes a similar verse in Revelation 7:15, but what is their point? Well, it is possible to interpret them both in terms of the elders and angels singing and praising God. This is entirely reasonable given that the same Greek verb latreuo is used for both service and worship. However, is it not also possible to see here echoes of another vision in which the Lamb is on his throne, with all his angels in attendance, and the nations before him? (Matt 25:31–46) On that occasion, reference is also made to those who served the King: "For I was hungry and you gave me something to eat, I was thirsty and you gave me something to drink, I was a stranger and you invited me in, I needed clothes and you clothed me, I was sick and you looked after me, I was in prison and you came to visit me." (Matt 25:35,36)

If we recall the point that the King makes on that occasion that "whatever you did for one of the least of these brothers of mine, you did for me" it then becomes possible to identify a very real continuum between our practical service of the poor now, and our worship in terms of sung praise in the age to come. Presumably that continuum is at least partly related to the notion that both service of the poor and praise of God stem from a desire to give due worth to whomever we encounter. If this is the case, then the challenge to us is to worship with the angels in heaven not so much by singing songs, but by feeding the hungry. In this strange paradox, heaven on earth is experienced most where we least expect it: amongst the destitute, for is that not where we find Jesus?

Justin Thacker, "Heaven," *What are we waiting for?*

5 ONE HOPE IN THE CITY

4. **The future is Jesus**. Christ's presence transforms the world into a new heaven and earth. As witnesses to his resurrection, we have experienced the power of new creation. As his people, we invite the world to become part of his new creation.

2.3
Here and now

At times when many people were hopeless, Isaiah and John promised hope unlimited. Their prophecies were not a ruse to cheer God's people up. They were written so that Israel and the church might live differently. Their poems and prose were to be remembered, performed, sung and narrated. By coming alive in his people, God's word brings life to the world. John is at particular pains to point out that what we do for God echoes throughout eternity. The church not only enjoys the feast of new creation but joins with the Holy Spirit in inviting the world to take part in the feast.

One of the things the church through history has been obsessed with is food. Like Israel before us, we recognise a meal as a powerful act. The meal table is where the family comes together, resources are shared and stories told. Sharing food is the perfect metaphor and mechanism for the life of God's people, so it is unsurprising that meals were a hallmark of Jesus' ministry. Even the simple way he broke bread and poured wine pointed towards the kingdom.

After his ascension, Jesus' disciples adopted the mealtime habits of their teacher. They became increasingly determined that no-one should be kept from their feasts, welcoming all comers regardless of race, creed, class, disability or moral position. This may not sound radical today, but Christ's first followers were Jews and their authorities did not welcome the breaking of the strict rules and routines of table fellowship.

The Holy Spirit confirmed to the disciples that Jesus was the hope of the world. As a result, his good news was for everyone. Having called the nations to join the party, there was no going back for the disciples. They were expelled from their synagogues but continued to meet for unstoppable dinner parties, which became what we know as church.

In considering how to follow the example of the early church one opportunity springs to mind immediately. Our increasingly global context is making it easier to have a party with people from several cultures. The world is as close as our doorstep, or mouse mat, for many of us. We have an unprecedented opportunity

space for notes

Comment: As Darrell Cosden has pointed out, John includes (Rev 21:4–6) our best achievements in his vision of the new Jerusalem. Those things we have done for God and his new creation will last for all eternity. "What we have done, our 'splendour', will be bought and put on display as part of the 'glory and honour of the nations'."
Darrell Cosden, "Eschatology goes to Work" in Stephen Holmes & Russell Rook (eds.), *What Are We Waiting For?* (Paternoster, Milton Keynes, 2008)

"… for my house will be called a house of prayer for all nations." The Sovereign LORD declares – he who gathers the exiles in Israel: "I will gather still others to them besides those already gathered."
Isaiah 56:7[b]–8

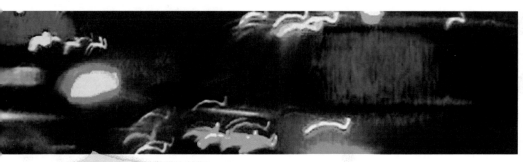

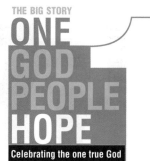

Hope Quote:

Daily bread

Eating is a moral act. Our tables need to include those who have been excluded…. We are what we eat. By our choices we shape our world. By our conversations, our talking , our praying, our liturgy, our justice, we live the Body of Christ and shape the reign of God.

David Andrews, "The Lord's Table, The World's Hunger" in Anne Y. Koester, *Liturgy and Justice* (Liturgical Press 2002)

Hope Quote:

Whose future?

The future belongs to those who give the next generation reason for hope.

Pierre Teilhard de Chardin (1881–1955), Jesuit priest, paleontologist, geologist, philosopher

Story of Hope:

Tommy

Tommy is an alcoholic who became involved in a church. His story is a powerful testimony to the church as a foretaste of God's eternal celebration and salvation.

"When I first came to church I remember I was bricking it. I thought how am I going to handle this, everybody preaching and all that, but it wasn't like that. It didn't take the first couple of sessions, probably just the first fifteen or twenty minutes, and I felt quite comfortable. I met some brilliant people, just brilliant amazing people, and I just thought these are so beautiful and they've got something like God or the Holy Spirit or something like that … I thought it might be interesting to grab a hold. For a while, when I was doing the Alpha sessions and when I was praying I'd go out of there feeling like twenty men. Usually it takes me a load of drink to feel like that to feel unbeatable, but I found myself without any alcohol or drugs feeling amazing. Then

I lost it. I can't believe how I felt at the time and how I want that back, because it was a good, good, feeling, and I had brilliant people around me. And I want to be involved in that again.

"I know there's a God, I see it in you all, that you people know God. I want to know God. I have found God when I was sober, but I don't find Him when I'm drinking, because my god is my bottle. But I know, when I'm sober again, which please God will be very soon, I know I'm going to go and run after Him again and chase after Him again, say my prayers again and read the bible. I adore so many of you in the church, I look at you and I think 'I want to be part of it'… I'm slightly envious… I would like to have that in my life, to be part of the church again."

Gary Bishop, *In Darkest England*

Hope Quote:

Common good

In the light of this, the most important political task of the church in the contemporary context is to, where possible, uphold the possibility of a common life shared with others and where necessary build bridges in order to foster common action in pursuit of the common good.

Luke Bretherton, *What are we waiting for?*

to celebrate God's hope and yet many of our churches are more mono-cultural than ever.

Let us think how our lives and churches can resemble new creation and the coming kingdom. Then let's consider how we can invite our friends and communities to attend the Messianic banquet that God has prepared for them. We'll need to share our lives with people from other faiths. Some of us will have to transform the ways and means of church life to make them more accessible. All of us will have to decide how to include those people who are currently excluded.

None of this is easy. Church history and statistics suggest it is difficult and painful. Isaiah and Revelation provide eternal hope, but neither says it will be easy. In fact, they promise exactly the opposite. And yet the rewards for succeeding are unimaginable. Our lives and families can provide a foretaste of the eat-as-much-as-you-like Messianic banquet. Our church communities can invite the nations of the world to enjoy the kingdom of God. Our efforts can impact God's plan to make all things new. Bill Hybels says, "The local church is the hope of the world." As far as the big story goes, this statement is both hard to question and hard to live up to.

Conclusion

Before we finish, let's review the ground we have covered.

Happily ever after

- ISAIAH, ADVENTURES IN THE IMPOSSIBLE: By allowing the Spirit to stretch his imagination and language, Isaiah describes the homecoming party that awaits Israel in the future. Prophecy not only brings hope that this will happen but a foretaste of what is to come.

- REVELATION, IN HEAVEN'S NAME WHAT'S GOING ON: John uses aspects of Isaiah's poetry to articulate his own revelation. Assuring them that he has not given up, God uses the trials of the church to bring about his perfect plan for history. God's people, as a result, are always on the winning side.

- APOCALYPSE NOW: every generation witnesses the changing times that history brings. The challenge is to hold true to Christ's kingship and live as wholly committed subjects of his kingdom regardless of the consequences.

Certain Rumour by Russell Rook
Join Cleopas and the disciple with no name as they wander down the Emmaus Road with the risen Jesus. This book retells the big story of the Bible from the vantage point of the resurrection, and proves that it is a short walk to hope.

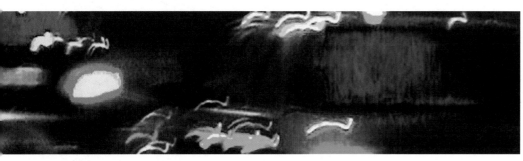

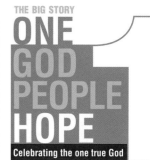

Hope Quote:

Good news

The good news of the resurrection is not, "You're going to heaven when you die," but rather, "Jesus is raised from the dead, therefore God's new creation has begun and we've got a job to do."

Tom Wright

Practical hope:

Getting involved

If you're keen for yourself and your church to get involved in bringing God's hope to your village, town or city, then Hope 08 could be a brilliant way of doing that in extremely practical ways.

The hope that we, the disciples of Jesus, profess is often hidden. The church is known by many as a dying, old-fashioned institution that rears its head in public only in order to point a wagging finger on moral issues.

The church does get involved in 'mission', but frequently limits itself to doing one thing over the course of one week in one particular location.

The idea for Hope 08 came from asking what would happen if the whole church could rise to the challenge of reaching the whole nation for a whole year – and beyond. What would be the result if in 2008 each community in the UK saw the life of Jesus displayed through the passion and actions of thousands upon thousands of Christians?

Hope08 is not an organisation fronted by Christian 'personalities'; it's a movement owned by the church in all her various expressions. The vision of Hope 08 is to encourage every church in the UK to:

Do more. However many hours of mission your church has notched up in previous years, if every church were to commit to doing more there would be a huge impact.

Do it in word and deed. We need to express the hope of the kingdom both through telling people about it and demonstrating it through our actions.

Do it together. By working together, churches in a neighbourhood can take a more strategic approach, and by seeking to work effectively alongside non-church organisations such as the police, the government and the media, the efforts of Hope 08 can be supported and have a far bigger impact.

With hundreds of churches, Christian organisations and denominations already on board, Hope 08 is something not to be missed. For more information, check out the website (www.hope08.com), which is constantly being updated with fresh ideas, new resources and more information – and allows users to give their feedback or add their own ideas too – or get hold of the *HOPE 08 Resource Manual*, which has hundreds of inspiring ideas that will allow your congregation to plan its year of mission in a way that suits your community best.

One Hope DVD course
A six-session DVD resource that brings expert input, provocative panel discussions and inspiring stories into small groups. Covering the themes of the Spring Harvest week, One Hope is a great opportunity to consolidate learning and share Spring Harvest back home.

The meal table

This table represents your own table that you eat around at home

In the various places write the names of (or draw) the people who have sat around your dining table over the last 12 months, including family, friends, neighbours, visitors and even strangers.

Heaven is a feast to which all are invited. How open has your home been to those who are not related to, connected to, or even similar to, you? Who would you like to make room for?

5 ONE HOPE IN THE CITY

At the end of the day

- JUDGMENT AND SALVATION: God will judge the world. The big story is consistent on this point, from beginning to end. There is no creature or aspect of creation, no event in time or space, that will escape judgment. In the same way, only God can save. In Jesus, we meet the creator, saviour and judge.

- HELL AND HEAVEN: The results of judgment and salvation are described by these doctrines. The church has various positions on hell. Underlying each position is the possibility of a Christless eternity. In the new heaven and earth, on the other hand, we shall witness a feast of eternal proportions. We must warn and excite the world about these respective futures.

- HERE AND NOW: As were the Israelites, we are given a foretaste of the Messianic banquet in the here and now. By endeavouring to live as new creations, God's ambassadors of hope to the world, we provide others with a chance to taste and see the infinite goodness of God's kingdom.

We have arrived at the end of God's big story. Isaiah and John have described the happiest of endings. Isaiah says God's people are called to a grand homecoming in a rebuilt Jerusalem. The feast that follows is so good that all creation rushes to join it. John shows the same celebration from an eternal perspective and locates it in the New Jerusalem, the capital of the new heaven and the new earth. The feast will last for all eternity. Here, everything is made new for once and for all.

What makes perfection possible?

The question, as we mentioned at the start, ought really to be, Who makes perfection possible? For God's hope for his creation is fulfilled by the same person through whom he made the world in the first place. As it was in the beginning, so it is in the end. Having made and sustained the world through Christ, God will perfect what he started by the life and work of his Son. Christ prepares the Messianic banquet by his life, death and resurrection. He provides the bread of life and the new wine of the kingdom. He makes all things new. His presence in the new Jerusalem negates any need for a temple, his life brings heaven and earth together as one.

Here we have again come across the key to all hope and to eschatology. Wherever Jesus is present, new creation comes to pass. For instance, his presence in our lives makes us into new creations, his Spirit in our churches transforms them into his body and his resurrection power in the world renews the created order. In Christ we have witnessed the end of the world, and the beginning of a happy eternal ever-after.

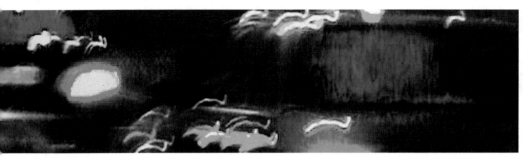

THE BIG STORY
ONE
GOD
PEOPLE
HOPE
Celebrating the one true God
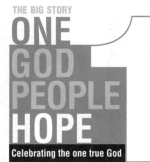

Recommended Reading

A Shorter Read

What Are We Waiting For?

Leading theologians and Christian thinkers discuss the issue of hope as it relates to theology, the Bible, the church and culture. The essays aim to provide a short and informative read.

"Heaven" by Justin Thacker

Looks at what we can say and experience of heaven in the here and now.

"Hell" by Robin Parry

Provides an introduction to one of Christianity's most difficult and uncomfortable subjects. Seeks to survey how the church has thought and taught about hell.

A Longer Read

Heaven… it's not the end of the world!: Biblical Promise of a New Earth by David Lawrence (Scripture Union 1995)

A thought-provoking book that provides a counter to the traditional view of heaven as a place of wispy spirits wearing golden crowns, clutching harps and singing Handel's *Hallelujah Chorus*. It examines what the Bible has to say about heaven and eternal life, concentrating on the biblical promise of a new Earth. Following the laying of biblical foundations, the author gives visions of life on the new Earth, asking what it may be really like. The final chapter explores the contemporary implications.

A Shorter Read

What You Always Wanted to Know About Heaven … but were Afraid to Ask by Catherine Butcher (CWR 2007)

Catherine looks at questions, such as 'How do I know heaven exists?' and 'What is heaven like?', and searches the Scriptures for what God tells us. Many questions about heaven, of course, cannot be answered but what God has revealed in his Word can give us a light and a hope to live by.

A Lighter Read

The Last Disciple by Hank Hanegraaff and Sigmund Brouwer (Tyndale House Publishers 2005)

A novel based on the book of Revelation, it provides a refreshingly different take to some of the other popular fictionalisations of the apocalypse.

A Deeper Read

The Theology of the Book of Revelation by Richard Bauckham (Cambridge University Press 1993)

The Book of Revelation is a work of profound theology, but its literary form makes it impenetrable to many modern readers and open to all kinds of misinterpretations. Bauckham explains how the imagery conveyed meaning in its original context and how the theology is inseparable from the literary structure and composition. The study concludes by highlighting Revelation's continuing relevance for today.

5 ONE HOPE IN THE CITY

Here, at the climax of God's big story, we can see the awesome scope of the church's mission.

- As HIS PEOPLE, we exist to witness to, and usher in, God's new creation.

- As HIS STORY, we live to enact and enable his plan to perfect the world.

- As HIS CHURCH, we are preparing to become his bride.

Spring Harvest exists to equip the church for action but it would be naive to suggest that any event could ever equip the church for her eternal vocation. If nothing else, we hope that the vision provided in these pages will encourage our hearts and stir us to greater levels of ministry and mission. Above all, we pray that an enlarged vision of God and his story in creation will provide us with new grounds for hope.

A Bigger Read

Big Boys Don't Cry by Nick Battle (Authentic Media 2007)
From humble beginnings, Nick seemed to have it all. His autobiography tells of rich rewards, working alongside the Spice Girls, a wife and two wonderful daughters. But a traumatic family illness left Nick devastated. Where was meaning in life when his whole world was falling apart?

A Book for all the Family

The Exile Road by Paul Kercal
A comic book about two children caught up in Israel's exile in Babylon that enables a family to journey through the themes and teaching of One Hope, and provides the perfect opportunity to share learning, prayer and action together.

Resources for Churches

The HOPE 2008 Resource Manual (www.hope08.com)

Not designed to be read from front to back, it covers a wide range of information that you can dip in and out of, reading only the chapters that concern you. If you're keen to get involved in this movement for a year-long mission effort, grab this well-designed and well-researched manual. It will give you loads of inspiration and ideas as well as pointing you towards hundreds of resources that have a good track record, without being prescriptive about how your church might bring hope to your part of the UK in 2008.